THE SHADOW OF A FIGURE OF LIGHT

The Archetype of the Alcoholic and the Journey to Enlightenment

by Cody Peterson

CHIRON PUBLICATIONS • ASHEVILLE, NORTH CAROLINA

www.ChironPublications.com

Cover image design by Abraham McCowan @chuckwallapress.
Used with permission
Interior design by Danijela Mijailovic
Printed primarily in the United States of America.

ISBN 978-1-68503-517-4 paperback
ISBN 978-1-68503-518-1 hardcover
ISBN 978-1-68503-521-1 electronic
ISBN 978-1-68503-519-8 limited edition paperback
ISBN 978-1-68503-520-4 limited edition hardcover

Library of Congress Cataloging-in-Publication Data Pending

C

Additional Praise for
The Shadow of a Figure of Light

This groundbreaking philosophical exploration seamlessly intertwines the wisdom of Alcoholics Anonymous with the profound insights of Jungian scholars like Erich Neumann and the mystical teachings of Meister Eckhart. Cody Peterson's book shines new light on the intriguing connection between Jung's visit to New Mexico with his very eccentric companion, a Renaissance Berkeley philosopher, who evoked in Jung his ongoing search for a relationship with a "Freudian" father figure. This thought-provoking book offers the reader a Jungian guide through the redemptive process of the 12-step program of AA which is at the core of the personal transformation of the alcoholic.

Indeed, the author goes further and credits "The archetype of *the Alcoholic* with helping to elucidate the birth of consciousness and the role that the opposing states of good and evil play in the quest for a coniunctio." This book is a must read, not just for Jungians, but for all practitioners and relatives who work and live with alcoholics.

--Ian Mc Cabe, Ph.D., Psy.D., is a Jungian Analyst and author of *Carl Jung and Alcoholics Anonymous*.

Peterson's new book *The Shadow of a Figure of Light: The Archetype of the Alcoholic and the Journey to Enlightenment* is a fascinating exploration of the back story history of AA, weaving mostly unknown threads of connection between Carl Jung, William James, Bill Wilson and an anthropologist named Jaime de Angelo, and how the archetypal underpinnings of one's own experience are the doorway to a true spirituality that leads to transformation, healing and freedom, not just for alcoholic and addicted individuals but for all of us. Peterson makes the vital connection between A.A.'s great psychological and spiritual wisdom and shows how these principles are available to and can benefit everyone in discovering their own personal myth. Peterson's personal knowledge and experience inform this work with an authenticity that rings true. He does an excellent job of linking the Twelve Steps and Jung's Individuation Process each step of the way. I don't agree with all of his conclusions, but I recommend this book wholeheartedly.

--David Schoen, Jungian Analyst and Author of *The War of the Gods in Addiction.*

Cody Peterson has written a book whose extension is deep, wide, and high. It rests on the solid foundations of careful scholarship and personal experience, it broadens our understanding of alcoholism beyond the reductive neuro-physiological explanations, and it elevates the vision of Bill Wilson and the Twelve Steps using the psycho-spiritual wisdom of C.G. Jung. It's a very readable book and highly to be recommended to anyone with an interest in the practical use of analytical psychology for addiction to anything, including the ego.

--Murray Stein, Ph.D., author of *The Mystery of Transformation.*

In this invigorating work, *The Shadow of a Figure of Light*, author Cody Peterson is able to infuse the C.G. Jung - Bill Wilson narrative with insights of indigenous spiritual investigations. The introduction of a Shamanic character, Jaime, allows the author to refract aspects Jung's personal journey and relationships through a Carlos Castaneda like lens. Peterson's insightful reflections on Wilson's methodology may prove helpful to those seeking to comprehend the shadowland of alcoholism.

--Jay Stinnett, A.A. Historian and Filmmaker of *Bill Wilson the Seeker.*

I dedicate this book to the only outstanding mind

with whom conversation isn't (usually) complicated—

Ming, my Magical Other.

Acknowledgments

Carl Gustav Jung's kind words to Bill Wilson, when the two corresponded in 1961, have stirred me deeply: "I conclude from your very decent and honest letter, that you have acquired a point of view above the misleading platitudes one usually hears about alcoholism." I know from personal experience that Jung's legacy of kindness toward the misfits of the world—people like me and perhaps Bill too—has been well preserved among his followers, as I have found the Jungian community equally encouraging and generous. Without their help, this book would not have materialized.

To Suzanne Reamy, my Jungian editor and friend, I owe the most heartfelt thanks: When we first met, I still didn't know what I was going to say, only that I needed to say something, and her patience and immense skill in helping me carve out a meaningful and coherent message is truly staggering! Dr. Steven Herrmann, who mentored me in the later stages of the process, is another person to whom I wish to give a special thanks: His graciousness in allowing me to publish the story of Jaime and Jung is one of the greatest gifts I have ever been given. The best one can hope for in terms of one's relationship to power is neutrality, but Dr. Herrmann has shown how it can be harnessed utterly for the good of another. On a similar note, I also want to thank the other Jungian scholars who provided me with testimonials and/or useful dialogue—as a person lacking in formal training and education, I appreciate how willing they were not just to read the manuscript, but to then put their neck on the line by telling their associates (and the rest of the world) that what I have written is worth the time it takes to read.

And though those in my own community have been much harder to impress, I owe a debt of gratitude to them especially. To begin with, all who received an earlier draft of the manuscript and expressed excitement about it—my inner circle—by giving me the most precious gift you have to offer, that of your time and attention, you instilled in me the courage I would need to finally shout from the rooftops as the book nears publication. Moreover, to the "trusted servants" who kindly read the manuscript in advance and provided a stamp of approval, I greatly appreciate you as well, for I recognize the wider audience your praise may generate in the years to come—thank you.

And finally, in addition to offering gratitude and praise to my long-suffering parents, my two amazing siblings, and my wonderful children, who helped me survive the hardships that my own plunge into the dark presented for all of us, I must give a special shout-out to my life-partner and her mom, whom I have often felt were the first people to really believe in me: Your support over the years has been immeasurable.

-Cody Peterson, 2024

"2000 years of Christianity can only be replaced by seeming equivalent. An ethical fraternity, with its mythical Nothing, not infused by an archaic-infantile driving force, is a pure vacuum and can never evoke in man the slightest trace of that age-old animal power which drives the migrating bird across the sea and without which no irresistible mass movement can come into being. ... I think we must give it time to infiltrate into people from many centers, to revivify among intellectuals a feeling for symbol and myth, ever so gently to transform Christ back into the soothsaying god of the vine, which he was, and in this way absorb those ecstatic instinctual forces of Christianity for the one purpose of making the cult and the sacred myth what they once were—a drunken feast of joy where man regained the ethos and holiness of an animal."

Carl Gustav Jung to Sigmund Freud, 1910

Table of Contents

C

Foreword

Everyone who opens the pages of *Alcoholics Anonymous* knows about the Twelve Step program, which has become a global organization with wide-ranging success for many kinds of addictions. *AA,* or the "Big Book" stitched together a series of tragic and successful stories illustrating with lucidity that when a person's fate is rearranged by a spiritual experience and devotion to a vocation, a light can emerge from the darkness of unfortunate events that transforms the individual's consciousness. What few people realize, even those interested in how people are freed from addiction, is that there is an untold story in the background of the movement of AA that began to take shape a few decades before the cofounder of the famous international movement, Bill Wilson, became sober in New York in 1934. This story is what is perhaps the most fascinating part of Mr. Peterson's book because it shows the interconnected web of transformative relationships that set the basic pattern for individual transformation and the organizational development we now celebrate. In his new and exciting work, Peterson uncovers for us, in a beautifully articulated volume, a story that is certain to add to our understanding of AA; if one takes the prescriptions in his book

1

seriously and, as the Big Book proposes, adopts a "design for living that really works," pursuing the path of one's own individuation, one may then discover one's central meaning and purpose in life.

When I began to read through the chapters of Peterson's book, a narrative gradually emerged that revealed an ancestral legacy that Wilson himself acknowledged as a debt of thanks to two of the founding fathers of modern psychology, William James and C.G. Jung. AA, now one of the largest organizations in the world, with memberships in virtually every part of the globe, did not emerge without any antecedents in America. There were spiritual leaders and teachers in the field of psychology who pointed Wilson to a way to awaken to his own Self-path so that he could bequeath his gift to humanity.

What Peterson points out brilliantly is that Wilson's spiritual awakening, an experience of inner Light that finally led him to put down the bottle once and for all came about through a succession of stories he'd heard from friends and perhaps especially from his reading of a seminal book by James, *The Varieties of Religious Experience.* James's writings on "religious conversions" were instrumental in Wilson's own quest toward sobriety and became what Peterson says was a "primary source of inspiration and understanding for the spiritual program he laid out in the Twelve Steps."

There are so many nuggets of wisdom in this book, written with a flair for prosody that is a sure sign of authenticity for Peterson's calling as a writer, for which the reader will be grateful. What readers may find to be the most insightful are Peterson's helpful contributions to the expanding field of Jungian analytical depth psychology, by way of some new information he presents that I have not seen published anywhere else. It is here that his prose catches fire and the spirit speaks through him for our enduring benefit.

The quintessentially American approach to spirituality that has spread around the world was a vocation James and Jung both wrote out of, and they taught their new vision of what it means to live a spiritual or symbolic life through their collected writings. Wilson caught this wave of American spirituality in a way the culture was ready for when the Big Book was published in 1939. Today, 85 years later, with the scholarship in Jamesian pragmatism and Jungian analytical psychology Peterson has managed to master, readers will be glad to imbibe his own spiritual offering.

There is something going on in the minds of members in Twelve Step groups that thirsts for this kind of knowledge and erudition about spiritual experiences as a solution to addiction, as well as for a plus, an addition, to what has been missing and is still to come. What comes through resonantly and resolutely in the overarching narrative is the voice of the teacher in Peterson. He tells us his own truth, in his own singular voice, and does not hesitate to challenge our preunderstandings by startling us with some of the missing pieces of the story of how AA was formed for the betterment of the world.

—Steven Herrmann, author of *William James and C.G. Jung: Doorways to the Self*

C

Introduction

Personal Roots

*"One does not become enlightened by imagining
figures of light, but by making the darkness conscious.
The latter procedure, however, is disagreeable
and therefore not popular."[1]*
C.G. Jung

Since earliest times, the path to enlightenment has been portrayed through symbolical stories of adventure, mythical tales that begin with a hero's plunge into the dark. Such tales are meant to be reflective of a pilgrimage into the parts of ourselves where we hope to discover the spiritual powers needed to bring healing and peace to our lives. And yet, while we usually think of "the darkness" as a barrier to our becoming enlightened, the energy that generates a truly life-changing

---

[1] C.G. Jung, *Alchemical Studies*, Bollingen Series, trans. by R.F C. Hull (Princeton, NJ: Princeton Univ. Press, 1983), para. 335. Hereafter, this specific volume is referred to as Jung, *CW*, vol. 13.

spiritual transformation is only found in the darkness, making our engagement with it of primary concern.

The process laid out in the Twelve Steps of Alcoholics Anonymous (AA), meant to bring about a spiritual awakening in its practitioners, is a modern template for enlightenment for all—"normies" and alcoholics alike. By guiding us into the darkness within our own psyche, the Steps move us towards a more meaningful connection to our figures of light. Yet, Jung reminds us that it's a journey few are cut out for: Making the darkness conscious is so unpopular, in fact, that nothing in our culture has prepared us for such an undertaking, either psychologically or spiritually. Thus, the Twelve Steps, like Jung's process of individuation, represent a journey of mythical proportions.

Bill Wilson, the cofounder of AA, was such an astute observer of the inner workings of his own mind that his book *Alcoholics Anonymous* (where he introduced the Twelve Steps) might be considered a masterpiece of modern psychology. In it, Wilson illuminates many of the more shadowy dynamics of the human psyche in a way that many of the world's best psychologists have been unable to match. Far from being either a prophet or a saint, Wilson himself was all too familiar with the darkness, part and parcel of a life lived in the throes of alcoholism and addiction. Like all who suffer such a fate, Wilson found himself face to face with a darkness so bedeviling that nothing could save him—not even his figures of Light. For people caught up in such an impossible dilemma, their only hope of survival is to make the darkness conscious. Though he wasn't a psychologist, Wilson was fascinated with human transformation and his method of recovery is a testament to his keen insight regarding psychic change. Quick to give credit where it was due, he referred to Carl Jung as an honorary cofounder of AA, a title he also gave to educator and psychologist William James, though he never met either of them and was at best only vaguely familiar with their vast scholarship. Still, their impact upon him was profound, for they each played a distinctive role in inspiring his own quest for psychological transformation.

In Part One, I present a fresh take on AA's historical roots. Beginning with William James's impact on Carl Jung's personal spiritual quest—an already controversial topic as the nature of James's profound influence on the Swiss doctor isn't well known, even among Jungians—I will demonstrate how it was actually Jung's own search for enlightenment, ignited by William James in 1909, that would have the most impact on Bill Wilson's sobriety and later formulation of the Twelve Steps, more so than any of his (or James's) theories.

With the help of Dr. Steven Herrmann, a respected San Francisco Bay area Jungian analyst and author who also loves local history, anthropology, and literature, I uncovered a significant element in the link between Carl Jung and his wealthy American patient Rowland Hazard, whom Wilson mentions early on in the text of *Alcoholics Anonymous*. Herrmann has graciously permitted me to cite an unpublished essay he penned in 2014 regarding Jung's pivotal (albeit short) friendship with another Bay area academic, a locally celebrated anthropologist and author named Jaime de Angulo, whose own darkness would end up serving a higher purpose than he could ever have imagined. It is well documented that de Angulo struggled with substance abuse, but what is far less known about him, and which Herrmann helped bring to light through his research, is that it was actually Jaime who guided Jung on his pivotal trip to Taos, New Mexico, in 1925, where he would visit with one of the Puebloan tribe's leaders. Along with de Angulo, that Taos elder, whom Jung would later refer to as "Mountain Lake" in his biography, opened up to Jung a perspective into "the mythic world" of the Native American, leading to the discovery of his "own myth."

De Angulo's friendship with Jung would play into the formulation of AA in two important ways. Firstly, it was Jaime's involvement with the shamans of certain Native American tribes, including the Ajumawi and the Taos, that led to the dawning of Jung's *personal myth*, a myth that is the direct antecedent to the spiritual journey Wilson presented in the Twelve Steps. Secondly, it was Jung's association with Jaime, who was what we might call "a live to die drunk," that sparked Jung's realization of an essential component required for recovery, the one that AA credits to him: in addition to complete abstinence, the alcoholic must have "a vital spiritual experience" in order to find meaningful and lasting sobriety. As I'll demonstrate, this insight likely came to Jung in large part as a result of his interactions with de Angulo, who gave Jung an unencumbered view into the spiritual nature of the disease of alcoholism, allowing him to intuit the very message he passed along to Rowland Hazard only a few months later.

I hope the reader will find the story of de Angulo and Jung as riveting as I did, though I would be remiss if I failed to acknowledge that in the retelling I did take some liberties interpreting how certain events might have been motivated, instances I point out clearly in the narrative. I believe that these educated guesses were inspired from my own intuition gleaned from many years of daily active membership in a Twelve Step fellowship, as well a lifetime of experience within the darkness of alcoholism and addiction (including more than ten years of "going in and out" trying to get clean and sober myself). Part of my *spiritual vocation* in recovery has been to "carry the message," as suggested in Step Twelve, and for more than a decade I have spent countless hours working with scores of newcomers. What one gains from actively participating in a Twelve Step program is access to a collective wisdom regarding psychological transformation that the outside world seems to know very little about—bought and paid for with our own pain and the blood of those who, like Jaime de Angulo, never got "the gift we were so freely given." Our sense of indebtedness to the Universe does not allow us to let those hard lessons go to waste, as they give us a keen insight into the nature of the disease that Jaime clearly suffered from, which we put to use in trying to help others. Because of this, I strongly believe that our accumulated acuity regarding addiction and recovery deserves a voice, a seat at the table, to participate in the ongoing discussion regarding the complexity of what, with Jung's help, we know to be at its core a spiritual illness. For while most of us are not professionals, our long experience has lent us the ability to discern about the alcoholic and/or drug addict's life far more than even they themselves can of a malady marked by a level of delusion that can take many years to unravel. Reading Jaime's story, I can't help but see him through the lens of my own experience—the reader can decide whether my interpretation feels right for them.

Having established a historical foundation in the first four chapters, ending with Wilson's own journey into sobriety and his revelation of the Twelve Steps, Part Two lays a framework for discussing the Twelve Steps from the perspective of "the mythic world," demonstrating how the Steps employ the same symbols and methods as the myths of antiquity. From there, I analyze the Steps from a Jungian perspective, first by flushing out Jung's own "psychological approach" to mythological symbols and then using a similar technique to examine the Steps and their impact within the psyche. By applying Jung's method of interpretation to the images and practices suggested in the Steps, a whole new psychospiritual landscape opens up, connecting our modern spiritual practice to the ancient traditions of religions around the world, revealing how the same fundamental dynamism that permeates the universe is the catalyst of spiritual growth that we find throughout our myths, including the Twelve Steps. With such a foundation in place, Part Three explores that most ancient of archetypes that Jung named the Trickster, comparing it with the modern shamanistic counterpart I call the archetype of *the Alcoholic*, an image reflective of the transformative power so apparent within the Twelve Step fellowships. Finally, in Part Four, I introduce Jung's concept of "the Self," showing how a similar notion emerged within Wilson's own consciousness, expressed through the shadow characters he unwittingly created in the Big Book as he elucidated a modern formula for psychological transformation. By overlaying the Twelve Steps with Jung's teachings, we see how a "coniunctio oppositorum"—the conjunction of the light and dark aspects of our nature—is central to the Twelve Steps and the essence of enlightenment.

Myths of Meaning

When Jung finally decided to write his biography, *Memories, Dreams, Reflections*, as an eighty-three year old man, he explained that he was undertaking to lay out a *personal myth*: "I can only 'tell stories,'" he writes, "whether or not the stories are 'true' is not the problem. The only question is whether what I tell is my fable, my truth."[2] In like manner, Bill Wilson had set out to reveal his own truth, having taken much broader strokes in relaying the story of AA's early days than most have realized. In 2019, William Schaberg, in his monumental history called *Writing the Big Book: The Creation of A.A.* posited,

> Bill's recounting of the facts is sometimes so wide of the mark that it can only be explained as willful, conscious mythmaking—the creation of a story specifically crafted to deliver a particularly clear image or an unmistakable lesson to the listener. All too often, Wilson's "this-is-what-happened" accounts must be understood and treated as nothing less than parables, as fables he fashioned to instill some hope in the still-suffering alcoholic or to provide an instructive, uncluttered story about the celebrated origins of Alcoholics Anonymous.[3]

---

[2] C.G. Jung, and Aniela Jaffé, *Memories, Dreams, Reflections* (New York: Vintage Books, 1989), p. 3. Hereafter *MDR*.

[3] William H. Schaberg, *Writing "The Big Book": The Creation of A. A.* (Las Vegas, NV: Central Recovery Press, 2019) pp. 1-3. Hereafter, *Writing the Big Book*.

In addition to illustrating how Jung's personal myth played into the emergence of the Twelve Steps, the aim of this book is to shine a light upon the spiritual nature of alcoholism and addiction, highlighting how the dangerous journey is, at its essence, a quest to discover meaning in the midst of a culture whose connection to its mythological images has all but vanished. And while "my own fable, my own truth" certainly forms the basis of what I present, out of respect for the Twelve Traditions, it is not my personal adventure that I share. Yet, such an approach proved to be the passageway through which the archetype of *the Alcoholic* would emerge—a paradoxical figure that reveals many subtleties regarding the nature of the transformation that we all seek. Rather than having relevance only to those who suffer from a particular facet of the psychospiritual disease of addiction, like all archetypes, *the Alcoholic* is woven into the fabric of the human psyche and can therefore help all of us to "make the darkness conscious." *The Alcoholic* is a personification of the *coniunctio oppositorum*, an image of wholeness whose function is to evoke a reconciliation of the opposites within us, fusing the darkest parts of our humanity with the figures of light we long to reconnect to, as we each traverse our own paths toward enlightenment.

Part One

The Mythological Mycelia
of the Twelve Steps

1

Psychological Roots

William James

Spiritual enlightenment is all but impossible to achieve without experienced guides to lead the way; yet, those who led Bill Wilson, the co-founder of Alcoholics Anonymous (AA), to his own "spiritual awakening"[1] were not priests, bishops, or rabbis, as one might expect. Rather, Wilson's spiritual transformation emerged with the help of two psychologists he never met, who themselves were riding the razor's edge of thought, in what was still a nascent branch of science. Thanks to their influence, Wilson was able to cultivate a unique perspective on spiritual experience, leading to his formulation of the Twelve Steps of Alcoholics Anonymous, an unquantifiable gift for today's troubled world. Wilson first published the Twelve Steps in his 1939 book *Alcoholics Anonymous* (colloquially known as the

---

[1] *Alcoholics Anonymous,* 1st ed. (New York City: Works Publishing Co., 1939), p. 60. Hereafter, *Alcoholics Anonymous*. See also *Alcoholics Anonymous: The Story of How Many Thousands of Men and Women Have Recovered from Alcoholism*, 4th ed. (New York City: Alcoholics Anonymous World Services, 2001). The page numbers between the first edition and the fourth edition are different, though the language remains almost verbatim throughout. I cite the first edition with fourth edition page numbers for ease of use for the reader, since earlier editions are harder to find. The first and second editions are in the public domain.

"Big Book"). And while his "Big Book" does contain references to some of the same symbols found in traditional religion, the method he portrayed came to him as the result of his concerted efforts to bypass religious convention and to adopt an approach to transformation that resembled the one being advanced by the psychologists.

What would ultimately coalesce into Wilson's own spiritual journey can be traced directly to the influence of one of these scientists in particular, the American psychologist and author William James, who was himself no stranger to the power of mystical experiences. James's father, Henry James Sr., experienced a religious conversion of his own, and dedicated his life to the service of the Christian God. Himself a published author, Henry James Sr. wrote many books on a variety of religious topics. Yet, young William was perhaps inspired even more by another writer, for just before his birth in 1842, his father became close friends with the esteemed Ralph Waldo Emerson, who had been blazing his own path to transcendence through his poetry and essays. Emerson became William's godfather, conferring a blessing upon him at his birth, destining him to carry forth the same mantle, to proclaim a new and quintessentially American approach to spirituality. According to Jungian author and analyst Steven Herrmann, it was a vocation for which James was well prepared. In his book *William James and C.G. Jung, Doorways to the Self*, Herrmann tells us that James spent much of his youth listening to his father's animated debates with Emerson on topics of religion, spirituality, and writing.[2]

---

[2] See Steven Herrmann, *William James and C.G. Jung: Doorways to the Self* (Oberlin, OH: Analytical Psychology Press, 2021). Hereafter *Doorways*.

Harvard, 1875

As a young man choosing an area of study, while James loved the arts, he pursued the sciences, namely chemistry and medicine. Born into privilege (Henry Sr. was a very wealthy businessman), William was afforded the luxury of traveling the world, learning from many renowned scientists and psychologists along the way, before he began his own career as a professor at Harvard in 1872, teaching physiology and philosophy. Three years into his tenure, in 1875, James offered a class on experimental psychology—a brand-new field of study and the first of its kind to be offered on American soil. In 1878, he presented the first doctorate degree in psychology in America to his student Stanley Hall, who would later become a pioneering educator himself and the first president of the American Psychological Association. James dedicated his significant insights to academia throughout his illustrious career, lecturing and writing, but he never treated patients one-on-one as a practitioner. He published many books on the subject of psychology, and in 1902, he put out his magnum opus, *The Varieties of Religious Experience*, based on a series of lectures he had given a few years prior in Europe, known as "The Gifford Lectures." *Varieties* was destined to change the course of history for both religion and psychology; after publication, it quickly became required reading for university

---

Most of the links in this chapter between Jung and James are a result of my extensive conversations with Dr. Herrmann, as well as a reading of his books and essays. I owe a debt of gratitude to Herrmann for his help in uncovering much of the history leading up to Jung's analysis of Rowland, which I describe in the next few chapters.

courses around the world, solidifying James's name among academic elites for generations to come.

The Varieties of Religious Experience, 1902

When James wrote *Varieties*, the field of modern psychology was still in its infancy, having been largely influenced by Sigmund Freud, whose own school of thought, "psycho-analysis," discounted religion, particularly in regard to its psychological impacts, asserting that due to its irrationality, religious experience was "just an illusion." On the other side of the Atlantic, William James, the leading thinker in the burgeoning science of experimental psychology in the U.S., took the opposite stance. Not only did he put stock in the validity and power of his own mystical experiences—many of which came to him while intoxicated on nitrous oxide[3]—through his research, James discovered that people from all walks of life have at times undergone profound psychological transformations that have had the earmarks of what he called "religious conversions." Yet most of these awakenings, James noticed, occurred outside of traditional religious channels, leading him to theorize that something inherent within the human psyche brings them about, quite apart from one's connection to any particular religious dogma. Examining the written and oral testimonies of many who had claimed to have such an experience, James realized that while their root cause cannot

---

[3] Michael Pollan, *How to Change Your Mind: What the New Science of Psychedelics Teaches Us about Consciousness, Dying, Addiction, Depression, and Transcendence* (New York: Penguin Press, 2018), p. 69. Hereafter, *How to Change Your Mind*.

be "proven" in the traditional scientific sense, the accounts of these religious awakenings should nonetheless be taken at face value and considered as "true" inasmuch as people who undergo them become empowered to change their behavior (and their lives). Thus, he realized that the *effects* of "religious conversions" can be empirically studied and verified while what *causes* them cannot. This insight led James to formulate the postulate he became most known for: *radical empiricism*, or the notion that the "truth" of any experience in life is solely dependent upon the meaning and value that one ascribes to it. *Radical empiricism* is a subjective approach to our experience of the world, counterintuitive to the previously held notion of *empiricism* employed by psychologists, derived from the natural scientists who base their definition of "truth" upon an objective notion of direct and measurable causes and effects. By contrast, *radical empiricism* attributes power to individual experience by injecting it with personal meaning, suggesting that the most powerful truths lie beyond our capacity to reproduce or explain.

James was in fact so impressed by the evidence that subjectively defined religious experiences had the ability to transform the psyche that he began to inextricably link the fields of religion and psychology. His resulting theories emphasized the need for an element of spirituality in the psychologist's approach to understanding human transformation, something he termed, "the psychology of religion." By the turn of the century, James had begun to singlehandedly change the course of both fields, defining the direction they each would take into the 20th century and beyond, for his book *Varieties* was a groundbreaking study on the power of religious images in treating many types of neuroses, not the least of which were alcoholism and drug addiction. Reading James's *Varieties* was instrumental in Bill Wilson's own quest toward continued sobriety, becoming a primary source of understanding and inspiration for the spiritual program he laid out in *Alcoholics Anonymous.*

Clark University, 1909

James's influence upon AA didn't end with *Varieties*, however. In 1909, he was invited by Stanley Hall, along with 26 of the world's foremost psychologists, to Clark University in Massachusetts to lecture on the science of psychology. Among those invited was the up-and-coming 34-year-old Carl Gustav Jung, already a favorite pupil of Sigmund Freud. Born in 1875 to a pastor of the Swiss Reformed church, Jung also started his career as a biological scientist and later transitioned into the growing field of psychology. In 1900, he began working at a renowned psychiatric hospital in Zürich, and by 1905 he was appointed its director. A gifted student, Jung set out to make a name for himself and began sending copies of his own books and reviews to Freud, hoping to get his attention. His boldness worked, and in 1907, he met Freud face to face, their initial conversation lasting 13 hours.

In 1909, the two men traveled together by boat to the United States to lecture at the conference at Clark, where James would also be presenting. Aboard the vessel, Freud asked Jung to interpret one of his dreams, though admitted to holding back a key part of the dream from his pupil for fear that it would tarnish his reputation. This incident revealed an uncomfortable dynamic that existed between the two men, perhaps marking the beginning of the end of their friendship. In *Doorways to the Self*, Herrmann points out that James's influence upon Jung exceeded what would have been considered entirely "professional," for when Jung met James at the conference a short time later, the draw he felt toward him was life-changing: James was 33 years Jung's elder, and his comportment toward Jung was markedly different from what he experienced from his former mentor in Freud, distinguishing the separation between him and Freud even more. In fact, meeting James struck Jung so deeply that he would write almost 50 years later, in a personal letter he composed in 1957, about how moved he was by the respect the wise old-timer afforded him:[4]

> Apart from the personal impression he made on me, I am indebted to him chiefly for his books. ... He was a distinguished personality and conversation with him was extremely pleasant. He was quite naturally without affectation and pomposity and answered my questions and interjections as though speaking to an equal. Unfortunately he was already ailing at the time so I could not press him too hard. Aside from Théodore Flournoy [one of Jung's earlier teachers and a close friend of James] he was the only outstanding mind with whom I could conduct an uncomplicated conversation. I therefore honor his memory and have always remembered the example he set me.[4]

---

[4] C. G. Jung, *Letters*, Bollingen Series, 95: 1-2. (Princeton, N.J.: Princeton University Press, 1973) vol. 2, p. 452. (Hereafter *Letters*)

Thus began the defining friendship between Jung and James. Sadly, James would pass within the year, though Jung made it a point to visit him once more on his way to Chicago a few months later. Yet, scholars have only recently started to investigate how deeply James shaped the course of Jung's life from that moment on—far more than previously considered. Eugene Taylor, a Harvard Divinity School scholar and lecturer on Jamesian psychology, began to piece together the link between James and Jung in the 1970s, writing several articles on the topic. Another scholar to notice the connection was one of Clark University's own history professors, William A. Koelsch, who recounted in 1984 that

> James was far more impressed with Jung [than with Freud], and the regard was mutual. They had a long evening conversation at Hall's house, discussing such topics as parapsychology and the psychology of religious experience, which James had opened up a few years before in his famous Gifford lectures and which Jung was to develop far more fully after his break with Freud.[5]

Sonu Shamdasani has also added to the conversation as a Jungian author who doggedly pursued the thread of James's influence on the Swiss psychiatrist. In 1999, after having

---

[5] William A. Koelsch, *Incredible Day Dream: Freud and Jung at Clark, 1909*. I owe a debt of gratitude to Billy N. for sharing this book with me and for encouraging me to pursue the James/Jung meeting at Clark from a Twelve Step perspective.

accessed and studied the manuscript of omitted sections from Jung's famous biography, *Memories, Dreams, Reflections,* Shamdasani published his findings in an essay he called "Memories, Dreams, Omissions." Referring to a precluded chapter on the influence of William James and Théodore Flournoy, Shamdasani quotes what appears to be a section of notes taken by Jung's biographer Aniela Jaffe: "[James] spoke to Jung without looking down on him; Jung felt that they had an excellent rapport ... that James was a model."[6] Steven Herrmann's book *Doorways to the Self* is among the most recent examining the James/Jung connection. In it, he makes clear that Jung, having been freshly impacted by his experience with Freud aboard the ship, saw the ailing James as a spiritual guru and left feeling personally inspired by James's own sense of direction and purpose, reconnecting to his spiritual vocation.[7]

And while nobody knows exactly what the two men discussed during the private meetings at Clark, what Jung likely appreciated most about James was his perspective on

---

[6] S. Shamdasani, "Memories, Dreams, Omissions" in P. Bishop (ed.), *Jung in Contexts: A Reader* (Taylor & Frances/Routledge, 1999), pp. 33-50. See also Walter Melo and Pedro H. Costa de Resende, "The Impact of James's Varieties of Religious Experience on Jung's Work," Journal of the American Psychological Association 23, no. 1 (2020): 62–76.

[7] See Herrmann, *Doorways*, 32-37. On page 33, Herrmann writes, "In 1913, Jung says he lost contact with his soul in 1902, which corresponds exactly with the publication date of James' masterpiece *The Varieties of Religious Experience*." Vocation is a notion that Jung taught which hearkens to a similar teaching from Paul the Apostle. See Jung's essay "The Development of the Personality," found in C. G. Jung, *Collected Works of C.G. Jung, Volume 17: Development of the Personality*, ed. R. F.C. Hull (Princeton University Press, 2014), paras. 284-323. See also Ephesians 4:1-3.

the healing properties of religious experience, or spirituality, in sharp contrast to the Freudian view, which held that the need for religion extends from unresolved trauma. Jung thus became sold on the Jamesian idea of "the psychology of religious experience," a phrase he would oft borrow from *Varieties,* which refers to the importance of a spiritual element in psychotherapy. It is somewhat surprising, therefore, that the extent of William James's influence on Jung's life has gone largely unnoticed, even by the majority of Jungians, for Jung himself quoted James many times throughout his career, even making him the subject of an entire chapter in his 1921 book *Psychological Types*. Jung adopted much of James's language too, as he developed his own approach to psychology.

Back in Europe, the dynamic between Jung and Freud began to worsen, and their friendship deteriorated. By 1913, Freud had had enough and sent a letter to Jung in which he carefully renumerated his defects, ending the relationship in such a way that both men would struggle to reconcile for the remainder of their lives: "I therefore propose that we abandon our personal relations entirely," wrote Freud.[8] They never spoke again. In turn, Jung began to develop his own school of scientific thought—"analytical psychology"—a model that echoed James's approach far more than Freud's. Yet, it was James's influence upon Jung's *personal* psychology that would lead to the creation of AA, for after he met James, Jung set out to discover his own part in "the divine drama

---

[8] Library of Congress, link as of 11/02/23: https://www.loc.gov/exhibits/freud/ex/131.html. Herrmann tells us that thanks to James's influence, Jung went on to "rediscover his soul" beginning shortly thereafter.

in which man plays,"[9] embarking upon a quest for what he would eventually call his *own myth*—the direct precursor to the spiritual journey that inspired Bill Wilson to compose the Twelve Steps.

---

[9] C. G. Jung, *Collected Works of C.G. Jung, Volume 11: Psychology and Religion: West and East*, ed. R. F.C. Hull (Princeton University Press, 2014), para. 226. Hereafter, Jung, *CW*, vol. 11.

2

The Spiritual Ancestors

Symbols of Transformation, 1912

Jung would eventually codify his psychological approach as the path to *individuation*[1]—the stated goal of his analytical method. His first real effort toward encompassing a personal myth came about when he published his book *Symbols of Transformation* in 1912, which heralded his broadening understanding of the role that symbolical imagery plays in the process of psychic change. When Jung republished *Symbols* in 1952, he rewrote the foreword, reminiscing upon the pivotal moment in his life when he first authored it, when it began to dawn on him that he had neglected to carefully examine his own mythological roots:

---

[1] James and Jung both (likely) borrowed the term *individuation* from Nietzsche. Jung used the term to describe the goal of psychological transformation which centers on the development of one's personal myth. Individuation involves the ego becoming differentiated from the collective and integrating split-off or disassociated aspects of the psyche, leading to a more fully developed personality. Ian McCabe, in his book *Carl Jung and Alcoholics Anonymous*, suggests that *individuation* equates to Bill Wilson's phrase "spiritual awakening." See Ian McCabe, *Carl Jung and Alcoholics Anonymous: The Twelve Steps as a Spiritual Journey of Individuation* (London: Karnac, 2015), p. 107.

Thus, this book [*Symbols of Transformation*] became a landmark, set up on the spot where two ways divided ... it laid down the [path I would follow for] the next few decades of my life. Hardly had I finished the manuscript when it struck me what it means to live with a myth, and what it means to live without one. ... The psyche is not of today; its ancestry goes back many millions of years. Individual consciousness is only the flower and the fruit of a season, sprung from the perennial rhizome beneath the earth; and it would find itself in better accord with the truth if it took the existence of the rhizome into its calculations. For the root matter is the mother of all things.

So I suspected that myth had a meaning which I was sure to miss if I lived outside it in the haze of my own speculations. I was driven to ask myself in all seriousness: "What is the myth you are living?" I found no answer to this question, and had to admit that I was not living with a myth, or even in a myth, but rather in an uncertain cloud of theoretical possibilities which I was beginning to regard with increasing distrust. ... So, in the most natural way, I took it upon myself to get to know "my" myth, and I regarded this as the task of tasks ... I simply had to know what unconscious or preconscious myth was forming me, from what rhizome I sprang.[2]

Ironically, Jung's "personal adventure"[3] into subterranean psychic depths, from whence his own myth would emerge, hinged upon his friendship with the famously eccentric Spaniard named Jaime de Angulo, a self-proclaimed drunkard who, in the tradition of Twelve Step anonymity, I will refer to as just "Jaime."[4] An influential Bay Area anthropologist, artist, and poet, Jaime's unique approach to anthropology, steeped in firsthand knowledge of the religious customs of certain Native American tribes, woven through his many poems, books, and essays, contributed to what would eventually be defined as counterculture in the San Francisco Bay Area decades later, making him a cult hero to this day. Dozens of books have been written about this "erratic genius," a crossdressing bisexual known to ride naked through the streets of Big Sur, bareback and brandishing a firearm.[5] And yet, with all that's been said about him, no one has linked Jaime to the emergence of AA, a connection which becomes apparent as we examine his association with Jung during the early to mid-1920s—10 years before Bill Wilson began his own journey into sobriety.

---

[2] C.G. Jung, *Collected Works of C.G. Jung, Volume 5: Symbols of Transformation*, ed. by R. F.C. Hull (Princeton University Press, 2014), pages xxiv-xiv. "Forward to the Fourth (Swiss) Edition." Hereafter Jung, *CW*, vol. 5.

[3] *Alcoholics Anonymous*, 60.

[4] Thanks to an unpublished paper from 2014, "Jaime de Angulo and C.G. Jung," by Steven Herrmann, wherein he examines the history of Jung's connection with Jaime, I have made been able to arrive at these conclusions. Hereafter, *de Angulo and Jung*.

[5] For an arrangement of Allen Ginsberg's thoughts about de Angulo, see an article entitled "Expansive Poetics" at www.allenginsberg.org.

Mythological Mycelia

After graduating from medical school at Johns Hopkins University in 1912, Jaime purchased a plot of land in a remote area east of Mount Shasta in far northern California with money from his recently estranged father. One day while working the land, he met some Ajumawi people (a branch of the Pit River Tribe) and, being a linguistics maestro, made fast friends with some of the tribe's people. Jaime was immediately attracted to the wildness of this ancient culture, feeling especially drawn to a young shaman among them named Sukmit. An accomplished writer, Jaime later revealed the intimacy of his relationship with Sukmit when he wrote of it: "How many ditches have we shared for a bed with a bottle of fire water?!"[6] The nature of his connection with Sukmit suggests that what Jaime had found among the American Indians went deeper than just a new method of anthropological inquiry, as important as that was: He bonded with the members of the tribe personally; he adopted their beliefs, and he became a lover and a friend. They were his people, and he was theirs. And while it's true that he would inadvertently stumble into a new method for anthropological research—"going native" as it came to be called—Herrmann writes that "what Jaime was really searching for was 'a religious outlook upon life,'"[7] exactly what Jung himself was seeking at the time.

Aided by Sukmit's knowledge of the tribe's religious rites, Jaime completely immersed himself in its mystical culture,

---

[6] Jaime de Angulo, "Afterword" by Guide de Angulo in *Indians in Overalls* (San Francisco: City Lights Books, 1990), p. 13. Hereafter *Indians*.
[7] Herrmann, *de Angulo and Jung*, 8.

explaining "[The Ajumawi] don't need so many ceremonies to understand the life of the world in trees, in the rivers, in the rocks. ... [They have] the 'wonder stuff' loose and free on tap."[8] Scholars have puzzled over Jaime's reference to "the wonder stuff," likely a variety of psychedelic mushroom called *Amanita pantherine*.[9] For, according to Ajumawi Headman Floyd Buckskin and his co-author, anthropologist Arlene Benson, "there is evidence that Ajumawi people living in the Fall River Valley southeast of Mount Shasta now use a yellow mushroom with hallucinogenic properties (A. *Pantherine*) for religious purposes, and have done so at least since the early part of the twentieth century."[10] Buckskin explains that this particular fungal species, which can be lethal at high doses, grows during the springtime from the root matter of birch and pine trees on the eastern slopes of Mount Shasta. Each year the shamans take a sacred pilgrimage to gather the mushrooms, drying them in small leather pouches for later use. Buckskin further elaborates:

---

[8] Guide de Angulo, *The Old Coyote of Big Sur: The Life of Jaime de Angulo* (Richmond, CA : CA Palm, 1995), pp. 226, 240-241. Hereafter, *Coyote*.

[9] In his unpublished essay, Herrmann writes that, "It's hard to know what the 'wonder stuff' on tap really was. But whatever it was, it was, from a feeling standpoint, the *real thing*: authentic religious experience that connected him to the Self in its non-dual aspect." This statement is interesting especially within the context of the alcoholic's longing to return to a "sense of ease and comfort which comes by taking a few drinks," as Dr. Silkworth writes. See *Alcoholics Anonymous,* xxviii.

[10] Floyd Buckskin and Arlene Benson, "The Contemporary Use of Psycho-active Mushrooms in Northern California," *Journal of California and Great Basin Anthropology*, 2005, vol. 25, No. 1, pp. 87-92. Hereafter, *Mushrooms*.

Indian doctors (shamans) would ingest these mushrooms during healing ceremonies to induce a trance that would allow the doctor to 'see' the shadow or spirit of the patient. The doctor also was able to see past, present, or future events in the life of the patient. Spirits of inanimate objects such as rocks, trees, mountains, or springs also can be seen in this manner.[11]

Needless to say, Jaime's tendency toward substance abuse would leave him completely enthralled by the tribe's religious rites, leading him to eventually come to an understanding of its myths, adopting its perspective of "the spirits of inanimate objects." Thus, while Carl Jung was gathering meaning as it emerged from the perennial rhizome within the human psyche, Jaime the drunkard had discovered it in a magic mushroom, which he came to believe didn't just grow from the roots of certain trees but was born out of "the mother" as a gift from "the spirits of Indian ancestors" who were themselves incarnated within "the soil, the trees, the rocks. In America the soil is teeming with the ghosts of Indians," he wrote, holding that "Americans will never find spiritual stability until they learn to recognize the Indians as their *spiritual* ancestors."[12] Such was the myth that Jaime found himself living, a far cry from his Catholic upbringing.

---

[11] Buckskin and Benson, *Mushrooms*, 89.
[12] Angulo, *Coyotes*, 248. Italics in original.

Celebrated by many as the first "hippie," another vocation certainly aided along by his alcoholism, Jaime sought to separate himself from the mainstream of so-called "civilized society," spending entire seasons in the mountains of northern California with his friends from the tribe, taking heavy doses of the psychedelic fungus (i.e., "tripping" on magic mushrooms), then smoking marijuana and drinking liquor to quiet his nerves on the comedown. Jaime would have been among the first to embark upon yet another field of academic research, though out of respect for the ancient culture, he kept the tribe's ceremonies a secret, as "the use of hallucinogenic mushrooms went underground, along with other Native American religious practices," as Benson and Buckskin report.[13] Nonetheless, the study of psychoactive drugs for psychiatric and medicinal purposes is one that is ongoing today, recently gaining traction even in some Jungian circles.[14] Over a three-year period in the late 1950s Bill Wilson participated in such research with Aldous Huxley, who wrote about his acid trips in his book *The Doors of Perception and Heaven and Hell*, and the best-selling author of religious philosophy, Gerald Heard. Ironically, the particular study they participated in examined the effects of the then-new drug LSD on alcoholism and depression.[15]

---

[13] Buckskin and Benson, *Mushrooms*, 91.

[14] For example, see *Psychedelics and Individuation: Essays by Jungian Analysts*, ed. by Leslie Stein and Lionel Corbett (Chiron Publications, 2023).

[15] See Don Lattin, *Distilled Spirits: Getting High, Then Sober, with a Famous Writer, a Forgotten Philosopher, and a Hopeless Drunk* (Berkeley: University of California Press, 2012). Wilson corresponded with Jung in 1961, writing the doctor two important letters. The first letter is well-known and will be examined in detail later in this book. Wilson's second letter is lesser-

With so much firsthand knowledge, Jaime easily made a name for himself in the anthropology scene in the Bay Area, and in 1920, he was hired to teach courses at UC Berkeley. He quickly drank his way out of what might have become a promising career when, lecturing one summer in the psychedelic mecca of Oaxaca, Mexico,[16] he stopped showing up for class, getting himself blackballed from the University of California altogether. But Jaime wasn't fond of what he called "museum anthropology," and after having been initiated into the Ajumawi's religious secrets, he made it his life's work to help preserve its ancient beliefs and customs. Jaime even poked fun at his former boss, Alfred Kroeber, the head of the department of anthropology at UC Berkeley, who gave Jaime the opportunity to become a

---

known; in it, he tells Jung about some of the insights he gleaned during his own psychedelic experiences. Of particular interest was Wilson's mention to Jung that "[Abram Hoffer and Humphrey Oswald] were no doubt the first physicians to see a spiritual significance in LSD. ... [They] believe that LSD temporarily triggers a change in blood chemistry that inhibits or reduces ego, thereby enabling more reality to be felt or seen." Wilson's own conception of the mystical powers of hallucinogenic drugs seems to be well correlated to Jaime's. Moreover, his mention of "more reality" appears to be in response to a comment in Jung's letter to Wilson (1961) in which he (Jung) states that the spiritual experience needed to combat alcoholism must come to one "in reality" rather than in a state of intoxication, however mystical it might have felt. Jung was unable to respond to Wilson's second letter, passing a short time after he received it. However, he did respond to a similar letter from Betty Eisner, who was also connected to Bill Wilson. That response can be found in C.G. Jung, *Letters*, vol. 2, pp. 382-383.

[16] Oaxaca is a place well-known for the "magic mushrooms" that grow there, with the first "recorded" incident of a Western "mushroom trip" having taken place there by R. Gordon Wasson and later published in Life magazine in 1957, thirty years after Jaime's visit. See: Pollan, *How to Change your Mind*, pp. 2, 108.

professor in the first place. After witnessing Jaime's antics in Mexico firsthand, Kroeber did everything he could to ensure Jaime never taught at UC again. Jaime's witty response reveals his undying loyalty to his indigenous friends: "Decent anthropologists don't associate with drunkards who go rolling in ditches with shamans."[17]

Jung and Jaime, 1923

When Jung met Jaime, he recognized that the nature of the vision quests Jaime had embarked upon in the wilderness was not much different from the one he was taking on the other side of the world, paradoxically in the highly civilized arena of modern science. While the means diverged, both were seeking a spiritual perspective on life: "Like Jung, Jaime was looking for his own personal myth, his own subjective story, his own way to truth."[18] It would turn out that Jung's fated meeting with Jaime would alter the course of history, marking the moment in time when a new myth took root within the perennial rhizome of our shared, collective unconscious—the Twelve Steps. His interactions with the beleaguered Spaniard greatly impacted Jung's own understanding of alcoholism and addiction, becoming the trove of wisdom from which he drew during his analysis of Rowland Hazard, who later influenced Bill Wilson's decision to go in search of a spiritual solution to alcoholism. Jaime's stories about his vision quests in the mountains helped Jung to flesh out an idea that he would continue to develop

---

[17] Gui de Angulo, "Afterword" in *Indians in Overalls,* (City Light Books, San Francisco. 1990), p. 53.

[18] Herrmann, *de Angulo and Jung*, 12.

over the course of his career: *For the alcoholic in particular, intoxication represents a spiritual experience*. Jung would write to Wilson a full 40 years later, in 1961, that the alcoholic's "craving for liquor is the equivalent … of the spiritual thirst of our being for wholeness … [or] for union with God."[19] Jung intuited that if Jaime's use of intoxicating substances was a spiritual quest unto itself, then the only way for him to overcome substance abuse would be to discover a sufficient substitute: to have "a vital, spiritual experience"[20] while in a state of abstinence. Jaime thus became the model for Jung's growing understanding of what is needed to treat addiction.

Jaime would have been a textbook example of the *spiritual thirst* inherent in alcoholics' behavior, evidenced by his attempts to forge a connection with the Divine through what we might call *an ego-less state of mind*, something like *nirvana*. Yet, coming from Western culture and being of nonnative descent prevented him from ever seeing the world as the Ajumawi, despite how close he came to it using drugs: "Never have I felt more power and peace. Is there any danger of my slipping back into a primitive condition of mind? Of becoming a real Indian? I don't think so."[21] As much as Jaime desired it, he recognized that his own background prohibited him from "becoming a real Indian." Jaime had read Jung's 1921 book *Psychological Types* and recognized in his native friends what Jung called a *primitive mindset*, referring to a religious attitude unique to indigenous peoples.[22] Such an ancient attitude is

---

[19] Jung, *Letters*, vol. 2, pp. 623-25.
[20] *Alcoholics Anonymous*, 26-27.
[21] Angulo, *Coyotes*, 223-24.
[22] "'Primitive' was an anthropological term that was in vogue at the time, and it was meant in a nonpejorative way to connote a person who lives out

inaccessible to Westerners, however, as it is impossible to understand the myth of another culture through the same psychic lens as one's own. Here in the West, we cannot simply disrobe from the cloak of our modern rationale, even with the help of repeated doses of psychoactives. The best we can do, Jung taught, is to develop our own psychological perspective of myth, whereby we learn to relate to mythological symbols as reflective of an inherent dynamic within our own psyche.

As for Jung, he was strongly against the use of mind-altering substances to "get there," writing that for him, "a new idea [was] intoxicating enough."[23] Nonetheless, he also recognized that for people like Jaime, the particular path that they take is the one that Fate has determined for them, that such a path might ultimately lead to enlightenment *if* one is willing to be as courageous going within as they have been plunging into the depths of a drug- or alcohol-induced trance. And while there can be no doubt that Jaime's particular style of searching for the truth among the Nature Gods as they manifested through consuming a yellow umbrella-capped mushroom certainly imbued his life with meaning, "without complimentary regressive analysis," as Herrmann points out, Jaime's lifestyle "produced a spiritual bypass, without much change to his post-

---

of the ground of the psyche in close contact with nature and who seeks thereby to stay in touch with a primal state of oneness." (Herrmann, *Jaime and Jung*, 3). See chapter nine for an in-depth examination of what Jung called "the primitive."

[23] C. G. Jung, *The Spirit in Man, Art, and Literature*, Bollingen Series 20 (Princeton, N.J.: Princeton University Press, 1995), para. 1465. (This is also known as volume 14 of the collected works, hereafter Jung, *CW*, vol. 14). In the letter Jung wrote to Betty Eisner, August 12, 1957, he explained that psychedelics tend to produce spiritual experiences that "cannot be integrated." See Jung, *Letters*, vol. 2, p. 382, 624.

traumatic character."[24] To have a full-blown spiritual awakening, rather than just a few mystical experiences, requires "an inside job," as one hears in Twelve Step meetings, for it is by seeing both one's religious beliefs *and* one's behaviors objectively that leads to a *permanent* shift in perspective. By adopting the ways of the shaman, Jaime had transformed his religious beliefs, but without a corresponding exploration of his personal traumatic history—what Wilson would later categorize in the Step Four inventory as *resentment, fear, and shame*—with the same rigor, fearlessness, and curiosity with which he participated in the ancient sacraments, Jaime would forever revert to being "driven by a hundred forms of fear, self-delusion, self-seeking, and self-pity"[25] whenever he came down off the mountain or the drugs. What Jaime really needed was a shaman to take him inward, to reveal to him the true state of his embattled soul, lest his unconscious reactions to his own ancient traumas continuously thwart his dream of one day abandoning the civilized world and leaving everything, including his ego, far behind: "to breathe freely … in oneness with nature."[26] Reading his history, a sad truth is revealed about Jaime that those of us who are members of a Twelve Step fellowship are all too familiar

---

[24] Herrmann, *Jaime and Jung*, 16. Keeping in mind that Dr. Herrmann never posited that Jaime used psychedelics, only that the "wonder stuff" represented "authentic religious experience," my position is that for some, intoxication does produce an authentic religious experience but eventuates, like every other form of spiritual practice, the possibility of spiritual bypass. Spiritual bypassing is defined as the tendency to seek a feeling of transcendent spiritual experience or a "spiritual high" while neglecting to face other, more painful tasks necessary for psychological development.

[25] *Alcoholics Anonymous*, 62.

[26] Angulo, *Coyotes*, 241.

with: His spiritual progress was constantly being interrupted by his unconscious outbursts toward his loved ones, fueled by self-pity, resentment, and fear. In the end, the nature of the spiritual illness from which Jaime suffered meant that his method for becoming egoless only inflated his ego more, countering his goal of attaining enlightenment, and like many alcoholics and addicts who find themselves split between two worlds, Jaime ultimately lost control over both.

It is unclear whether Jung himself ever tried to be such an internal guide for Jaime—scholars disagree on whether Jung got him "on the couch" or not. More importantly for our discussion, however, is the fact Jung learned firsthand from Jaime that he was powerless to help him overcome substance abuse—even if Jaime had wanted to be helped—that *certain types* of alcoholics would need something more than what regressive analysis could offer in order to achieve long-term sobriety. By the time they met, Jung had heard all about Jaime's adoption of Native American beliefs, as well as his alcoholism, from his patient Cary, Jaime's ex-wife. She had spent significant time accompanying Jaime in the foothills of Mount Shasta but realized, after their daughter was born, that the unpredictable, dangerous lifestyle Jaime pursued in the mountains was not conducive to child rearing. By 1922, Jaime and Cary had gotten a divorce and were fighting a custody battle, for which she needed help navigating and sought out Jung. So, when Jung first heard of Jaime's romps in the woods, his scientific interest was piqued about how the Spanish alcoholic, in the midst of his own search for meaning, had gathered more extensive firsthand knowledge of the Ajumawi's secret religious rites than any outsider ever had. Hoping to help Jaime with his substance abuse, as well as to satisfy his own curiosity regarding the

American Indians' ancient beliefs, Jung invited Jaime to his fabled estate in Switzerland, known as Bollingen Tower—a castlelike structure that Jung had begun constructing a couple of years earlier—his own religious retreat in the woods.

During Jamie's weeklong visit, their first in-person encounter, the two men camped on an island of the lake adjacent to the house, where they exchanged ideas regarding "primitive thought from a linguistics point of view" and Jung shared his "mythological and philosophical perspectives."[27] Jung must have been impressed by Jaime's primitive skill set while the two men lived among the rocks and trees for a week, as Jaime built shelter and lit fire with the techniques his native friends had taught him. However, an emergency back in California cut their time short: Jaime's house had burned down, and with it all of his books, journals, and academic papers, though it wouldn't be the last time that the alcoholic's life would be reduced to ashes. Jaime returned to the States right away to begin rebuilding, and on the eve of the new year, 1924, Jung graciously sent him $500 to help him get back on his feet—equivalent to about $10,000 today—so he could continue studying the creation myth of the Ajumawi.[28]

---

[27] D. Bair, *Jung: A Biography*. (New York: Bay Back Books, 2004), p. 334.

[28] In his essay, Herrmann mentions that this is more money than Jung ever gave to anyone else during his life. Readers in the Twelve Step fellowships may wonder, as I have, whether Jung might have been what is called an "untreated Al-anon." If so, it would help explain why he sent Jaime large amounts of money on a number of occasions. But it would also help to explain Jung's intuitive sense of the alcoholic affliction—unmatched by anyone who doesn't suffer from the disease personally.

3

Mother Earth, Father Sun

Back on the West Coast, Jaime befriended a member of the Taos Puebloan tribe from New Mexico, a man named Tony Lujan, who was wintering in the Bay Area with his partner Mable Dodge. It turned out to be of particular significance that the Taos Tribe had begun an outreach program a couple of years earlier, inviting influential Western writers to attend some of the tribe's sacred ceremonies and to speak with the elders about how their traditions had come under attack by the U.S. government's devastating campaign to systematically eradicate the ancient culture and religion of the Native American.[1] Jaime's friend D.H. Lawrence, the famous author, had been invited the previous year, and since Jaime, a respected anthropologist with skill in native tongues and musicology, was already privy to certain underground native religious customs, they extended to him the honor of an invitation as well. Jaime traveled to Taos in 1924, with Tony as

---

[1] In the late 19th century, the United States government began sending native youths to boarding schools where they were forbidden to wear native garb, speak native language, and practice native religion. The policy was known as "Kill the Indian, save the man." This and many other destructive tactics were being used to try and stamp out native religion and culture.

his guide, to be initiated into some of the Taos tribe's rituals. He was soon dismayed, however, to find out that the religious rites of the Taos were far more "civilized" than those of the "California Indians."[2] Jaime had continued to correspond with his ex-wife Cary, who was still in Switzerland with Jung, and after his initial trip to Taos, he wrote to her explaining that

> Without knowing it I wanted black magic from [Tony]. He, not being a magician, quietly refused. He says 'I have only spirituality to give you. Take it or leave it—but don't give me headaches.' Jung said all that to me, last summer, but I wasn't ripe to understand, then. I am more so, now.[3]

Typical of most alcoholics, Jaime had no interest in exploring spirituality as he believed "the civilized" practiced it. And while we don't know the details of what Jaime and Jung discussed in Bollingen, it appears that Jung may have encouraged Jaime to seek out a different kind of mystical experience than he had been having, perhaps one a little more suited to sate his spiritual thirst in civilized life. Jaime had certainly found *some* spiritual truth through what Tony dubbed "black magic," but for alcoholics to find lasting peace, they must also discover

---

[2] Jaime wrote to Cary: "I may never find anything of interest to my special line of research, among the Pueblo Indians. I feel they are too civilized. My Indians are the California tribes. They don't need so many ceremonies to understand the life of the world in trees, in the rivers, in the rocks… [They have] the 'wonder stuff' loose and free on tap." *Coyote*, pp. 226, 240-241.
[3] Angulo, *Coyotes*, 219-220, 226.

meaning in the kind of "spirituality" Tony referred to, but which Jaime was either unable or unwilling to pursue. Jaime felt a sense of impending doom, as many practicing alcoholics do, as if he needed to strike a balance within his psyche, lest he be split apart by the "paradoxical knife-edge" separating the two worlds he was caught between, as he wrote to Cary. Jaime longed for the kind of mystical connection that could sustain him in both arenas—in the wilderness, among the natives—and back home with his new wife and children, giving him the wherewithal to support them, emotionally and otherwise—something he always struggled to do.

Cary knew Jaime all too well and read the letter to Jung, who responded with an elaboration on the metaphor of the knife-edge that demonstrates his innate understanding of the tremendous polarity that alcoholics are trapped in: "In short, you cannot content yourself to live on a paradoxical knife-edge, [the myth you adopt] has to symbolize the suitable fusion of the pairs of opposites in a way that makes it possible for you to function in a civilized society without shutting out the primitive."[4] And while each of us faces our own spiritual quandary, the knife-edge that threatens alcoholics eventually backs them into an impossible dilemma, "from which there is no return through human aid," as Bill Wilson would write more than a decade later, explaining that they have "but two alternatives: One [is] to go on to the bitter end, blotting out the consciousness of [their] intolerable situation as best [they] can]; and the other, to accept spiritual help."[5]

---

[4] Angulo, *Coyotes*, 224.
[5] *Alcoholics Anonymous*, 25.

Jung Goes to Taos, 1925

Jaime was neither prepared to integrate the light nor did he want their help. Then, in January of 1925, on a whim Jung decided to come to the U.S., and while he was here, Jaime had the intuitive thought that he should take Jung to Taos. There was one problem, however, for the Taos were very selective about whom they invited and hesitated to let the Swiss doctor come, even though Jaime had given Tony his word that the tribe could trust Jung to help their cause:

> I won't ask anyone [about the Taos tribe's secrets]. They can tell me if they want to. You know I want to know and you know I will not publish anything. You know I will not tell anyone except that man in Switzerland, and he will never tell, but he can do good with it, he can do things with it. I am going to Taos as your friend. I will not look at anything. I will not ask any questions.[6]

Unable to make the final decision as to whether Jung could visit the Pueblo, Tony introduced Jaime to one of the chiefs, Antonio Mirabal, whose native name is "Mountain Lake." Thankfully, Jaime was able to convince Mirabal that Jung's world renown as the founder of analytical psychology and accomplished author qualified him to help them transmit the important message regarding the existential threat to their

---

[6] Angulo, *Coyote*, 235.

people and their way of life, and in January of 1925, Jung began his own pilgrimage to Taos. His first stop was on the south rim of Grand Canyon, where he then sent a telegram to Jaime from El Tovar Lodge, instructing him to rent a car and pick him up, "no expense to [Jaime]."[7] A few days later, the two of them embarked upon a classic American road trip, south from Grand Canyon to Flagstaff, then east down the San Francisco mountain range and out through the spacious desert toward Gallup, Albuquerque, and Taos, passing through the corridor that conjoined ancient and modern worlds—the now famous U.S. Highway 66—under construction at the time.[8] Over the course of their extended road trip through the desolate canyons of the American southwest, Jung would glean even more firsthand knowledge of the stark realities that a practicing alcoholic must face, even one who saw the world through a mythical lens, as Jaime did.

Upon arriving at Taos, "the roof of the world," Jung and Mirabal met up to talk about the Puebloan myth. Jung shared some of the religious secrets that Mountain Lake told him, though out of respect for the ancient culture, he only divulged those that the Medicine Man had asked him to. In his autobiography, *Memories, Dreams, Reflections*, Jung revealed how impactful that meeting was for him:

---

[7] Gui de Angulo, *Jaime in Taos: The Taos Papers of Jaime de Angulo* (San Francisco: City Light Books, 1985), 87. Hereafter, *Taos*.

[8] Herrmann saw the spaciousness of the American Southwest as highly influential for Jung, explaining that "Spaciousness is part of a larger analytic frame for [Jungians]. Eckhart and James and Jung all point to the way to such a broadening." Herrmann, *Doorways*, 173.

After a prolonged silence [Mountain Lake] continued, "The Americans want to stamp out our religion. Why can they not let us alone? What we do, we do not only for ourselves but for the Americans also. Yes, we do it for the whole world. Everyone benefits by it."

I could observe from his excitement that he was alluding to some extremely important element of his religion. I therefore asked him: "You think, then, that what you do in your religion benefits the whole world?" He replied with great animation, "Of course. If we did not do it, what would become of the world?" And with a significant gesture he pointed to the sun.

I felt that we were approaching extremely delicate ground here, verging on the mysteries of the tribe. "After all," he said, "we are a people who live on the roof of the world; we are the sons of Father Sun, and with our religion we daily help our father to go across the sky. We do this not only for ourselves, but for the whole world. If we were to cease practicing our religion, in ten years the sun would no longer rise. Then it would be night forever."

I then realized on what the "dignity," the tranquil composure of the individual Indian, was founded. It springs from his being a son of the sun; his life is cosmologically meaningful, for he helps the father and preserver of all life in his daily rise and descent. If we set against

> this our own self-justifications, the meaning of
> our own lives as it is formulated by our reason,
> we cannot help but see our poverty. Out
> of sheer envy we are obliged to smile at the
> Indians' naïveté and to plume ourselves on our
> cleverness; for otherwise we would discover
> how impoverished and down at the heels we
> are. Knowledge does not enrich us; it removes
> us more and more from the mythic world in
> which we were once at home by right of birth.[9]

While the stories Mountain Lake told had struck a chord, Jaime too, in his own way, had filled the role of Shaman for Jung by introducing him to the symbolical world of the Native American.[10] The traditions embodied by these two men—the way Jaime was enamored of the mysteries of Mother Earth and how Mountain Lake's generational religious traditions honored Father Sun—further demonstrated to Jung the antimonial powers of the unconscious as it manifests through living myth. Mountain Lake in particular was to become Jung's

---

[9] Jung, *MDR*, pp. 251-52.

[10] Not only did Jaime inform Jung's understanding of addiction, but he also helped Jung on his journey to discover his own myth. In Chapter Eleven, I demonstrate that in modern times the ancient energy of the shaman has constellated through what I call the archetype of *the Alcoholic*. If Jung unconsciously identified with *the archetype of the Alcoholic* by way of his somewhat inappropriate relationship with Jaime, then perhaps his interactions with this dark side of the archetypal shaman energy is the very thing that allowed him to ultimately tap into its light-giving power in Taos and Africa. In that case, both Jung's method of individuation as well as Wilson's Twelve Steps stemmed from that source—the archetype of *the Alcoholic*.

own spiritual ancestor, for the elder's tale left Jung wondering what kind of story might link him to the Moon, the Sun, the Stars, the Trees, the Rocks, and the Rivers. Longing for his own cosmologically meaningful connection, Jung couldn't help but recognize his own spiritual poverty, in spite of his vast store of knowledge about religion and psychology. He had wanted the kind of wealth that only comes from having such a perspective of one's place in "the mythic world" as he saw in these characters, who reflected to him an image of the barren landscape he had come to discern in his own psyche.

Jung Goes to Africa, 1925-26

Leaving Taos, Jaime returned to life in the Bay Area, but Jung's quest to tap into his own mythological roots continued. He took a trip to Africa only a couple of months later, and one afternoon while on safari in Athi Plains, Kenya, he wandered off, away from the group, to meditate alone upon the quiet, wind-swept savannah that stretched out like an ancient ocean before him.[11] As he sat there watching "gigantic herds of gazelle, antelope, [and] zebra ... moving forward like slow rivers," the legend of the Taos came back to him:

> There the cosmic meaning of consciousness
> became overwhelmingly clear to me. "What

---

[11] Jung went to Africa with a close friend of his, Helton Baynes, who paid for the trip. Cary, Jaime's ex-wife, was to go along with them, for she had recently married Baynes. She was still Jung's patient, too, and Jaime would soon lose the custody battle with her over their daughter, Ximena. Thus, Jaime's memory stayed with Jung throughout the entire course of his trip to Africa and his subsequent meeting with Rowland.

nature leaves imperfect, the art perfects," say the alchemists. Man, I, in an invisible act of creation put the stamp of perfection on the world by giving it objective existence. This act we usually ascribe to the Creator alone, without considering that in so doing we view life as a machine calculated down to the last detail, which, along with the human psyche, runs on senselessly, obeying foreknown and predetermined rules. In such a cheerless clockwork fantasy there is no drama of man, world, and God; there is no "new day" leading to "new shores," but only the dreariness of calculated processes. My old Pueblo friend came to my mind. He thought that the raison d'être of his pueblo had been to help their father, the sun, to cross the sky each day. I had envied him for the fullness of meaning in that belief, and had been looking about without hope for a myth of our own. Now I knew what it was...that man is indispensable for the completion of creation; that, in fact, he himself is the second creator of the world, who alone has given to the world its objective existence—without which, unheard, unseen, silently eating, giving birth, dying, heads nodding through hundreds of millions of years, it would have gone on in the profoundest night of non-being down to its unknown end. Human consciousness created objective existence and meaning, and man found his indispensable place in the great process of being.[12]

In Africa, Jung finally discovered what he had been looking for the previous decade, the "preconscious myth" that was forming him. In a moment of inspiration, *a myth of expanding consciousness* opened before him, a psychological reflection of the divine drama that the Taos participated in. The Sun for them was a religious symbol, and for Jung it represented the light of consciousness. So, for the Taos, to assist the Sun rising over the horizon reflects the work of the individuated ego, the vehicle of consciousness, as it sheds an ever-expanding light upon the world, giving it objective existence. In Jung's myth, it is the enlightened ego that is called to help humankind awaken from the slumber of mythlessness that most are trapped in, like the Americans in Mountain Lake's dream. For Jung, this realization allowed him to find his place in the great process; it was his own "act of creation" that revealed his part in the divine drama.

The Twelve Steps are based on a similar *myth of expanding consciousness*, described in Step Eleven as "[improved] conscious contact with God, as we understood Him."[13] By seeking to increase our conscious connection with God, and helping others do the same, we begin to understand the profound insight that Jung described, which came to him in Taos and Africa, that without conscious contact with the human ego, the Earth would have remained unheard, unseen,

---

[12] Jung, *MDR*, p. 255-56.
[13] *Alcoholics Anonymous*, 60.

and unfulfilled, as it was for eons before it began to awaken to its own existence through human perception. Jaime hoped that by participating in the myth of the Ajumawi, he might come to enjoy such an undifferentiated state, fully identified with his surroundings, suspended in *participation mystique*, when the part of the psyche that perceives itself as a separate and distinct entity is dormant. Jaime believed that such an egoless condition was the goal, as many of us do, having been taught that the ego is so deficient we'd be better off to rid ourselves of it entirely. Yet, Jung came to recognize that the enlightened ego is the only entity in the universe that can impart meaning and value to the Universe itself, and so rather than seeking to abandon our ego, perhaps a better course of action for us to take would be to try and awaken it from its unconscious dream, to discover and live out our own *myth of expanding consciousness*, as Jung did.

Though Jaime had cultivated a unique and important relationship to Mother Nature, in order for him to find an enduring connection to Spirit, he needed to integrate the dark energies of the unconscious that had him captivated, walking his own psyche (or soul) into the light of awareness and love. As usually happens with alcoholics who never get sober, the world became an increasingly difficult place for Jaime. He and Jung ceased communicating soon after their trip to Taos; when Jaime finally lost the custody battle with Cary, he began to nurse a lifelong resentment toward the doctor, blaming Jung for his misfortunes rather than looking at where he might have been to blame himself. In a horrible car accident in 1933, Jaime drove off a cliff near Big Sur, California, killing his 9-year-old son and seriously injuring himself—likely under the influence when it happened. Ten years later, Jaime's second wife, Nancy, left him, and after attempting suicide while residing alone in Berkeley, he moved to San Francisco, where he was diagnosed with prostate cancer shortly thereafter. Jaime's life came to an end much like every other typical alcoholic, well short of the potential which Jung, Tony, and countless others had perceived in him.

Jaime stood at the door knocking, as it were, never realizing that he was holding the key and could have let himself in. Had he been able to heed the advice of Jung or Tony, perhaps the ensuing chain of events, including Wilson's own sobriety and the creation of the Twelve Steps, would not have come about as it did. By introducing Jaime into the story of AA's creation myth, perhaps we might honor him as the first of many martyrs for the spiritual way of life that he unwittingly helped to create. Indeed, the Twelve Step fellowships can say of Jaime, as we do of the other countless friends we've lost to the disease, that "he died so that we could live." For if Jung hadn't gotten to know Jaime's struggles so intimately, he may never have recognized that regressive analysis, and therapy in general, cannot get a real alcoholic sober, regardless of how beneficial it is to them otherwise. More than anyone else in Jung's career, it was Jaime who revealed to him that the alcoholic needs something more than what a scientific method could produce. Jaime helped Jung gain an appreciation of what Wilson would later classify as Step One: "We admitted we were powerless over alcohol, that our lives had become unmanageable."[14] Yet, it was Jung's own psychological journey

---

[14] *Alcoholics Anonymous*, 59.

toward a connection to Spirit, sparked by William James over a decade earlier, that revealed to him the mystery of Step Two: "[We] came to believe that a power greater than ourselves could restore us to sanity."[15] Fate wove their stories together, setting the stage for the transformation of innumerable lives of alcoholics, addicts, and their families, even though James, Jaime, and Jung never got to fully enjoy its fruit.

Jaime died in 1950, leaving us to wonder whether he had ever heard of the strange new spiritual movement from the East Coast called Alcoholics Anonymous, which had been introduced to the Bay Area as early as 1939 and was well established by the mid-'40s, with dozens of regular weekly meetings throughout the region. And while Jaime's death symbolizes the last of the generations of alcoholic and addict families who didn't have a solution, Jaime's life truly marked the beginning of a new era, when a religious culture known as "recovery" would span the globe and the hard lessons he transmitted to Jung about the disease of alcoholism and addiction would be put to proper use by sober alcoholics and addicts in more than a hundred countries worldwide.

---

[15] *Alcoholics Anonymous,* 28, 59.

4

Myths of Expanding Consciousness

Jung and Rowland, May 1926

By the time he left Africa, Jung's discovery of *a myth of expanding consciousness* had spread into an all-consuming flame that would fuel his vocation for the rest of his life. Forty years after his pivotal trips to the Taos Pueblo and Kenya, on the first page of his biography *Memories, Dreams, Reflections*, Jung wrote: "Thus it is that I have now undertaken, in my eighty-third year, to tell my personal myth. I can only make direct statements, only 'tell stories.' Whether or not the stories are 'true' is not the problem. The only question is whether what I tell is my fable, my truth."[1] Although he waited until the end of his life to share his "personal myth" with the world, it would begin to inspire alcoholics and addicts much sooner, for it exemplified the individual's quest for spiritual connection that became the cornerstone of Alcoholics Anonymous.

The first inroad came by way of another unlikely candidate, an alcoholic of a similar ilk as Jaime—the wealthy "American businessman" mentioned in the Big Book, who had tried every means to curb his alcoholism and finally

---

[1] Jung, *MDR,* 3.

sought out Jung's help—his patient, Rowland Hazard.[2] It was Jung's message to Rowland that would eventually inspire Bill Wilson, effecting the creation of AA and the Twelve Steps. And while the timing of Hazard's treatment had always been presumed to have occurred in 1931,[3] with the help of recently unearthed letters and journals from the Hazards and their extended family, multiple researchers have placed Hazard's monthlong analysis with Jung beginning just eight weeks after the psychiatrist returned home from Africa, in May of 1926.[4] Although the articles and essays written to date about the connection among Jung, Hazard, and Wilson have focused mainly on establishing its historicity, Amy Colwell Bluhm, in her paper "Verification of C.G. Jung's Analysis of Rowland Hazard and the History of Alcoholics Anonymous" remarks that pinpointing the timing of Hazard's analysis positions us to understand Jung's influence on Twelve Step ideology:

> Now that the year of Rowland Hazard's initial
> analysis has been clarified through primary

---

[2] See *Alcoholics Anonymous*, 26-28.

[3] See Amy Colwell Bluhm, "Verification of C.G. Jung's Analysis of Rowland Hazard and the History of Alcoholics Anonymous," American Psychological Association 2006, Vol. 9, No. 4, 313–324. In Wilson's second correspondence with Jung, from March of 1961, he mentioned that Rowland's treatment took place in 1931, which seems to be at least part of what caused the confusion for so long.

[4] Cora Finch and Amy Colwell Bluhm each explored the historical connections that linked Hazard, Jung, and Wilson in their 2007-2008 essays, "Stellar Fire: Carl Jung, A New England Family, and the Risk of Anecdote" (Finch) and "Verification of C.G. Jung's Analysis of Rowland Hazard and the History of Alcoholics Anonymous" (Bluhm). Much of the historical narrative in this chapter was taken from Finch's essay.

source material, there is a fresh opportunity to draw out Jung's historical effect on Alcoholics Anonymous. … Future work could approach the material by constructing an exposition of Jung's theory as it emerged historically including the point at which Rowland Hazard stepped into the analytical hour and began an interface with Jung's emerging theory.[5]

Examining Jung's influence upon the creation of the Twelve Steps necessitates that we take into account his association with Jaime, including their pilgrimage to New Mexico, as well as Jung's subsequent trip to Africa, just weeks before meeting Rowland—none of which has ever been considered together within the context of Jung's connection with AA. With such an influx of insight, gleaned from the fresh discovery of his own "personal myth," Jung's analysis of Hazard took on new color. Consequently, more than any of his theories regarding psychological transformation, it was Jung's own spiritual quest that seems to have had the most appreciable impact on the adventure Wilson later set down in the Big Book. The combination of Jung's search for a personal myth, along with his firsthand knowledge of Jaime's heartbreaking dilemma, allowed Jung to be so frank with Rowland when the two met a short time later:

[5] Amy Colwell Bluhm, "Verification of C.G. Jung's Analysis of Rowland Hazard and the History of Alcoholics Anonymous," American Psychological Association 2006, Vol. 9, No. 4, 324.

Exceptions to cases such as yours have been occurring since early times. Here and there, once in a while, alcoholics have had what are called vital spiritual experiences. To me these occurrences are phenomena. They appear to be in the nature of huge emotional displacements and rearrangements. Ideas, emotions, and attitudes which were once the guiding forces of the lives of these men are suddenly cast to one side, and a completely new set of conceptions and motives begin to dominate them. In fact, I have been trying to produce some such emotional rearrangement within you. With many individuals the methods which I employed are successful, but I have never been successful with an alcoholic of your description.[6]

Jung's experience with Jaime in particular had shaped his perspective on the spiritual nature of the disease, illuminating for him the most counterintuitive yet most important thing that he could have conveyed to the American: *Analysis wouldn't be sufficient to get him sober; he would need "a vital, spiritual experience" to counteract his alcoholism.* And while the conversation we have above is Wilson's secondhand account of an interaction between Jung and Rowland, the

---

[6] *Alcoholics Anonymous*, 27. Keep in mind that Wilson's account of the conversation between Jung and Hazard was passed down to him not from Rowland himself, but thirdhand from Ebby, probably in 1934 or 1935.

underlying message corresponds with Jung's beliefs about alcoholism as they took shape throughout his career, that such an inward shift could not be evoked by anything other than a supraordinate power. Jung went on to tell Rowland that "while [his] religious convictions were good, they did not spell the vital, spiritual experience,"[7] emphasizing that the connection needs to be so *original* and *primary* that one cannot find it within the confines of conventional religious dogma, East or West. In short, Rowland would need to forge a *personal myth*, as Jung had.

It is plausible that Jung had Jaime in mind when he commented that he had "never been successful" with an alcoholic of Rowland's variety. Jung probably could have guessed, judging from Jaime's example, that his time with Rowland would have very little impact on his long-term bid for sobriety, and he would have been right, for Wilson tells us that Rowland relapsed shortly after leaving Jung's care. Because his financial situation allowed him to move frequently between cities around the world, Hazard immediately began taking what Twelve Steppers call "geographics," chasing the delusion that a new venue might somehow recast his old character and behaviors. Undoubtedly in a desperate search for what we can only guess Jung spoke of during their time together, in 1927 Rowland took a trip to the African savannah along the same route Jung had the previous year. Then, after a long stay in the hospital and a hazy stint in London, in 1929, Hazard purchased 2,000 acres of pristine land in New Mexico and moved there to construct a house, as Jung had done

---

[7] *Alcoholics Anonymous*, 27.

in Bollingen. The timing of Hazard's decision to go to both Africa and New Mexico suggests that Jung's prescription for Rowland must have included him disclosing a fair amount of his "personal equation"[8]—it seems plausible that Jung told Rowland about his own comings to in those sacred places as he tried to explain to the alcoholic that he would need to experience something similar if he expected to recover.

Rowland and the Oxford Group, 1932

As Bill would write a few years later, "alcohol is a subtle foe,"[9] and in spite of Hazard's best efforts to outrun it, in 1932, he wound up in the hospital yet again, this time back in New York. Encouraged by members of his family, he joined the First Century Christian Fellowship, or the Oxford Group, an evangelical movement established in 1921 by Frank Buchman—a friend of the Hazards—and for a while it worked. Rowland became an active member in the group, sent by Buchman around the U.S., Canada, and Europe to tell the miraculous story of his conversion from alcoholic degenerate to servant of Christ.[10] And while Oxford Group spirituality is a far cry from what is now practiced in AA, the Group holds a special place in AA's history as it played a huge role in the early sobriety of many of the first-generation members, including

---

[8] Jung, *CW*, vol. 5, pages xxiv-xiv. "Forward to the Fourth (Swiss) Edition."
[9] *Alcoholics Anonymous*, 85.
[10] Jungians generally believe that Jung mentioned Rowland in his 1939 talk to the London Guild for Pastoral Psychology, found in Jung, *CW*, vol. 18, paras. 620-21. The talk is titled "The Symbolic Life." See: C.G. Jung, *Collected Works of C.G. Jung, Volume 18: The Symbolic Life*, ed. R. F.C. Hull. Vol. 11. (Princeton University Press, 2024)

Bill Wilson and his co-founder, "Doctor Bob," the proctologist from Akron, Ohio, whom Wilson helped get sober on June 10, 1935—the day chosen for AA's official anniversary. Thanks to the Oxford Group, Wilson became connected to Rowland, who delivered the Jungian myth from which Wilson would eventually forge his own conception—the journey toward a power greater than himself—as he finally harvested the fruits of Jung's work with Jaime.

Cora Finch, in an essay called "Stellar Fire: Carl Jung, A New England Family, and the Risk of Anecdote," provides the missing link between Jung, Hazard, and Wilson, describing how Rowland and a few of his Oxford Group friends brought Ebby Thacher in, the man who would help Bill Wilson sober up later that year:

> The primary connection between Bill Wilson and Rowland Hazard was their mutual friend, Edwin (Ebby) Thacher. Ebby met Rowland in Manchester, Vermont during the summer of 1934, when Cebra Graves introduced them. Cebra had become involved with the Group earlier that summer [and] persuaded Rowland to help Ebby stay away from alcohol. Ebby stopped drinking and later moved to the Calvary Mission in New York City under Rowland's guidance. Ebby paid a visit to his old friend Bill Wilson, took him to a service at Calvary Mission, and later brought him into the Oxford Group. Ebby maintained a close relationship with Rowland over the next year,

traveling to New Mexico with him during the summer of 1935. No doubt some of what Ebby learned was passed on to Bill.[11]

After Ebby moved to New York City and started attending Oxford Group meetings, he learned of the dire situation of one of his longtime friends, another drunk named Bill Wilson. Like Jaime and Hazard, Wilson was the type of alcoholic who, despite the strongest desire to do so, was incapable of staying sober for any length of time, having arrived at a state of acute psychosis that few people understand and even fewer survive. Awash in a raging sea of booze, Wilson was dying from alcoholism; he would later describe it as an experience of "incomprehensible demoralization," having "arrive[d] at the jumping off place," he "wished for the end"[12] but like many who have suffered so, was too afraid of dying to kill himself.

Bill Wilson Gets Sober, 1934

Tuesday, December 11, 1934, a few weeks after Ebby's initial visit with him, Wilson, for the fourth time in a little over a year, checked himself into Towns Hospital, a leading treatment facility in New York City. There, he was placed under the care of Dr. William D. Silkworth, an expert physician who had treated him before. And while Silkworth suggested complete abstinence, his method had lacked the other key component required for a drunkard like Wilson to achieve

---

[11] Cora Finch, "Stellar Fire: Carl Jung, A New England Family, and the Risk of Anecdote."

[12] See *Alcoholics Anonymous*, 30, 152.

long-term sobriety—"the vital, spiritual experience" that Jung prescribed to Rowland. Ebby visited Bill in the hospital to familiarize him with some of the actions that the Oxford Group suggested he take if he expected to stay sober, the first inkling of the program that Bill would later formulate into the Twelve Steps. These principles included humbly offering himself to God, admitting his faults, and setting things right to the best of his ability. After Ebby left, while Wilson sat alone in the hospital, he realized that he "couldn't believe in the God that Ebby believed in" and cried out in all sincerity, "If there is a God, let him show himself to me!"[13] What happened next would come to be known as Wilson's "white light experience," out of which the entire Twelve Step movement grew. Wilson explained that as an answer to his prayer, he felt the presence of God fill his room, blowing through him like a fresh mountain breeze. He admits that the experience he had in Towns was so moving that he came to believe in God, a conception that would redefine itself for the rest of his life.

That same night Wilson's own spiritual vocation was born, as a vision of a society of sober drunks from coast to coast came to him. The next day Ebby showed back up to visit, toting a copy of William James's *The Varieties of Religious Experience* and (presumably) a story to tell Bill about Rowland Hazard's important conversations with the world famous psychologist Carl Jung regarding a phenomenon he called "a vital spiritual experience." Wilson was able to use what he

---

[13] Alcoholics Anonymous, ed. *"Pass It on": The Story of Bill Wilson and How the A.A. Message Reached the World* (New York: Alcoholics Anonymous World Services, 1984), p, 120. Hereafter *Pass It On*.

had learned from the Oxford Group, along with information he gleaned from James and Jung, as a foundation for what would become the Twelve Steps. And despite playing such a key role in its formulation, Hazard never did join Alcoholics Anonymous; nevertheless, his association with Jung became foundational in Wilson's understanding of the nature of the inward journey that the alcoholic must brave in order to recover.

Wilson's keen intuition told him that the most effective thing he could do for himself in order to maintain his own sobriety was to work intensively with other alcoholics, which he set out to do immediately. During the formative years of the fellowship, Wilson spoke with hundreds of drunks to help them get sober, but only a handful actually did each year, many of whom practiced an early version of the ideas that he (thankfully) decided to set down in ink. Unable to find employment, Wilson spent a lot of effort trying to raise money to set up a nationwide chain of rehabilitation hospitals, groping through the dark still unable to clearly make out the true nature of his calling—though his incessant work with other drunks enabled him to miraculously stay sober himself. In March of 1938, Wilson abruptly left the Oxford Group, having come to the realization that certain aspects of its convention weren't helpful to him and the other drunks he was trying to help. Meanwhile, a group of sober alcoholics continued to meet at his small Brooklyn apartment every Tuesday evening, drinking coffee, praying together, and sharing "experience, strength, and hope." Unable to raise capital for a chain of rehabilitation hospitals, it was in May of 1938, after much convincing from Frank Amos, one of John D.

Rockefeller's closest associates, that Wilson began writing a book, which he published in April of 1939.[14] And while he tried to get input and feedback from the other members of the little band of sober brothers (and one sister)—the majority of whom lived in Akron and were still devout Oxford Groupers— most were uninterested, even discouraging the idea, believing that Wilson, still unemployed, was trying to turn a profit on the spiritual principles they were practicing. Nevertheless, a few of them (reluctantly) contributed their personal stories, to be included in the back of the book.

Undaunted, Wilson pressed along, and that growing group of sober men and women eventually formed into the fellowship of Alcoholics Anonymous, officially named after the Big Book was published. And while AA was the first Twelve Step fellowship, hundreds of other sister fellowships would follow, each implementing their own version of the Twelve Steps; in nearly every one, the Steps have been carried over almost verbatim, becoming the spiritual foundation for millions of people worldwide—a *myth of expanding consciousness* which has now spread to every corner of the globe.

The Twelve Steps, 1939

With his formulation of the Twelve Steps, Wilson's own *personal myth* began to take shape. And though the years since the Big Book was written have brought a great many scientific and technological advancements, theologically speaking, Western culture has barely shifted. When Wilson introduced

---

[14] Schaberg, *Writing the Big Book*, 108, 188.

the Twelve Steps to the world, he had no idea of the profound impact it would have due to its broad adoption by generations to come. Yet, the way the Steps were expressed through him highlights how religious symbols emanate from the depths of the human psyche and how powerful it can be to discover oneself living within one's own myth. Nowhere is this clearer than in historian William Schaberg's recently published book, *Writing the Big Book: The Creation of A.A.*, where he sheds light on Wilson's process. Examining how the Big Book was created, Schaberg provides a composite rendering of the author's own recollections, compiled from some of Wilson's recorded talks at various AA meetings through the years. Quoting Wilson's own words, Schaberg pieces together the moment Wilson's myth emerged from beyond the horizon of consciousness:

> With a speed that was astonishing, considering my jangled emotions, I completed the first draft in perhaps half an hour. The words kept right on coming. When I reached a stopping point, I numbered the new Steps and saw they added up to twelve. Somehow this number seemed significant. Without any special rhyme or reason I connected them with the twelve apostles. I had started with the idea that we needed to broaden and deepen the basic concepts of the program by making them more explicit, but that was the only idea I had when I began to write. The most amazing thing about this experience was that I didn't seem to be thinking at all as I wrote. The words just

flowed out of me and I've come to believe that the Steps must have been inspired—because I wasn't in the least bit inspired myself while I was writing them. I have no idea why I wrote the Steps down in that particular order or why they were worded as they were. For reasons unknown to me, my new formulation not only mentioned God several times throughout, but I had moved Him right up to the very beginning of the Steps. Whatever, I didn't pay much attention to that at the time. I actually thought it all sounded pretty good.[15]

Bill's own journey from the darkness of active alcoholism into the realm of recovery and light began the night he checked himself into Towns, and it would continue for the rest of his life. While it is true that he borrowed some of the tenets of the Twelve Steps from the Oxford Group, Wilson's *myth of expanding consciousness,* so poignantly expressed through the Steps, was based almost exclusively on his own experience, as Schaberg handily demonstrates throughout his book. The Steps are a set of religious symbols far more profound than anything Wilson's conscious mind could have produced at the time, stemming from a divine synthesis of his own spiritual intuition and experience.[16] A symbolical outpouring that can

---

[15] Schaberg, *Writing the Big Book,* 442-43.

[16] Jung, who was no stranger to the creation of a myth, confirms that it is "impossible to create a living symbol, i.e., one that is pregnant with meaning, from known associations. For what is thus produced never contains more than was put into it." C. G. Jung, Gerhard Adler, and R.

be described as *archetypal*, the Steps are a blueprint that millions continue to admire and emulate, a paradigm for spiritual transformation in the modern world.

Myth is a function of the universal human experience of transformation, the collective dream of our unconscious longing for wholeness. Moreover, the mythlessness Jung felt prior to his own life-altering experiences in New Mexico and Africa is the same mythlessness that resonates through Western culture today, out of which the Twelve Steps sprang. Investigating the historical thread that connects William James, Carl Jung, Jaime de Angulo, Mountain Lake, Rowland Hazard, and Bill Wilson allows us to understand more about the nature of the "preconscious rhizome" from which each of our own *personal myths* are waiting to emerge. Taking the Steps, we tap into the well of human spirituality and link ourselves to our spiritual ancestors, including the Ajumawi and Taos peoples, bringing a much needed measure of spiritual stability into our lives, as Jaime recognized was needed.[17] Taking the Steps, we begin to create a *myth of expanding consciousness* for ourselves by shining an ever increasing light of awareness upon our unconscious delusions, defenses, and defects of character, coming full circle when we share the tale of our own adventure into "the mythic world" with those who are still suffering as we once did.

F. C. Hull, *Collected Works of C.G. Jung, Volume 6: Psychological Types* (Princeton: Princeton University Press, 2014), para. 817.

[17] "In America the soil is teeming with the ghosts of Indians," Jaime wrote, "Americans will never find spiritual stability until they learn to recognize the Indians as their *spiritual* ancestors." (De Angulo, *Coyotes*, 248).

The following are the Twelve Steps as written by Bill Wilson and published in chapter five of the book *Alcoholics Anonymous* in 1939:

Here are the steps we took, which are suggested as a program of recovery:

1. We admitted we were powerless over alcohol— that our lives had become unmanageable.
2. Came to believe that a Power greater than ourselves could restore us to sanity.
3. Made a decision to turn our will and our lives over to the care of God as we understood Him.
4. Made a searching and fearless moral inventory of ourselves.
5. Admitted to God, to ourselves, and to another human being the exact nature of our wrongs.
6. Were entirely ready to have God remove all these defects of character.
7. Humbly asked Him to remove our shortcomings.
8. Made a list of all persons we had harmed, and became willing to make amends to them all.
9. Made direct amends to such people wherever possible, except when to do so would injure them or others.
10. Continued to take personal inventory and when we were wrong promptly admitted it.
11. Sought through prayer and meditation to improve our conscious contact with God as we understood Him, praying only for knowledge of his will for us and the power to carry that out.

12. Having had a spiritual awakening as the result of these steps, we tried to carry this message to alcoholics and to practice these principles in all our affairs.[18]

---

[18] *Alcoholics Anonymous,* 59-60.

Part Two

A Psychological Approach
to the Twelve Step Myth

5

Living Myths and Dying Gods

Having explored the circuitous path of how the lives of James, Jung, and Wilson intersected, forming a passageway through which the Twelve Steps could emerge, we're now ready to take a deep dive into the nature of the journey within. For as Jung was observing psychological transformation from an analytical perspective, Wilson, channeling his own style of Jamesian pragmatism, fashioned a simple set of actions to set it in motion. By drawing parallels between the two approaches, we position ourselves to better understand the mystery of our own spiritual awakening. The journey of the Steps, like that of Jungian analysis, is one that spans the breadth of our being, from our highest spiritual aspirations to our lowest, most depraved secrets; where these converge, there is the potential for us to discover our own *personal myth*, to close in on the elusive goal of enlightenment.

Jung saw myth as a window into human psychology, and viewing the Twelve Steps as a "modern myth" allows us to apply Jungian theory to unpack them. The difference between the Steps and the myths of ancient cultures is that in the Steps, the highly symbolical film has been wiped away, revealing a clearer picture of the psychology at work in spiritual awakening—exactly what Jung and James studied throughout their careers. But one could argue that since symbolism is the language of myth, removing a symbolical layer or two from a religious statement should disqualify it from being classified as such. After all, anyone who has attended a Twelve Step meeting will have noticed among the misaligned rows of fold-up chairs strewn about the coffee-stained floors, a lack of rites, idols, or altars that are typical of places of worship, ancient or modern. In fact, in "the rooms" where Twelve Step meetings are held, there's almost nothing resembling either religion or mythology aside from a cheap vinyl banner printed with those 12 enshrined tenants—never mind the motley crew professing to have found a genuine spiritual awakening as a direct result of practicing them.

Furthermore, those who have familiarized themselves with the book *Alcoholics Anonymous* know that it too lacks the mythos we've come to expect from our religious texts. The Big Book tells no story of the creation of the world, renders no universal fall of mankind, and preaches no plan of redemption from that fall. In it, there are no portrayals of burning bushes, miraculous sea crossings, or appearances of angels carrying direct messages from God. Most notably, neither the Big Book nor any of the Twelve Step fellowships have anything whatsoever to say about the afterlife—aside from mentioning that those who die clean and sober "go off to the big meeting in the sky," which frankly sounds more like hell to rest of the world. But joking aside, while the Big Book does have plenty to say about God, religion, and spirituality, its interpretation of such seems rather philistine compared to how other religious traditions have consecrated their doctrines and creeds, at least on the surface. Yet, those whose lives have been transformed grant to it far more canonical significance than they do "the other big book," the telling phrase one might hear used in reference to the Bible, for what a person finds "in the rooms" seems to be of far more spiritual significance than anything else they have come across in years of desperate searching. And since no one ever aspired to become a member of a Twelve Step group, any lodes of spiritual insights contained therein still remain largely untapped by the broader public— most have concluded that the Big Book couldn't be much more than an instruction manual on how to stay away from "boozing and using," seeing that Twelve Step meetings are just a place for alcoholics and addicts to go for peer support.

However, comparing Wilson's "program of action" to Jung's very dense epistemology, with its basis in all types of mythological symbology, we see that the Twelve Steps is in fact a clear, precise, and unparalleled expression of a modern *myth of expanding consciousness*. Examining Twelve Step customs and practices closely, including the extensive oral tradition that accompanies them, we'll see that indeed the mythos typically associated with the ancient tales does in fact permeate the Twelve Steps, discovered within the psychological process they present, meant to lead one ever deeper into the realm of the unconscious. Still, what follows is bound to raise the hackles of more than a few in academia, and ironically even a few Jungians, who may be resistant to giving equal footing to the ideas of a man lacking in formal education and training, as Bill Wilson was, as they would to Jung. Yet, based on the Twelve Steps's widespread success, it would be folly to exclude them from any serious consideration of psychological transformation in the West today. Then again, even some of the old-timers in the fellowships, themselves the entrusted bearers of the torch of Twelve Step methodology, will balk at what follows, averse to the idea that their spiritual program should be exposed to an in-depth inquiry from what will probably feel like a sterilized scientific perspective—as if the mystery of their spiritual awakening could be more clearly elucidated by examining it under a metaphorical microscope. What they may not realize, however, is how lucky they are to have been initiated into a mystical tradition so penetrating that none but C.G. Jung himself could really circumscribe it.

The Anonymous Alcoholic

The goal of every spiritual tradition (since long before humans even started crushing grapes) has been to inspire personal transformation for the members of the tribe or the community most in need, and on that basis the Steps are a beacon of light. Still, the path to enlightenment lies hidden in places that most don't care (or dare) to look. Such a journey requires one to heed closely the interior world, for the only way to "get there," Jung taught, is from within:

> Every great experience in life, every profound conflict, evokes the accumulated treasure of these [mythical] images and brings about their inner constellation. But they become accessible to consciousness only when the individual possesses so much self-awareness and power of understanding that he also reflects on what

> he experiences instead of just living it blindly.
> In the latter event they actually live the myth
> and the symbol without knowing it.[1]

Despite being rooted in modern psychology, the Twelve Steps nevertheless encompass many of the same images from which other world myths have derived. Like Jung's analytical method, by showing us how to engage in a process of self-reflection, the Steps help us to unlock the power that such images evoke *whether we consider ourselves religious or not*. Presenting concepts that feel familiar to us, the Steps have become an effective daily spiritual practice for millions of people from every religious background and from all walks of life—a far cry from the ragged group of destitute drunks who banded together in the 1930s, in New York and Akron, to form Alcoholics Anonymous. In many cases, those who have "recovered from the seemingly hopeless state of mind and body"[2] that alcoholism and addiction present are no longer cursed to "live the myth and the symbol without knowing it," for the Steps have empowered them to make conscious what previously remained hidden within the shadows of their own psyche.

Therefore, studying the Twelve Steps is a worthy endeavor for everyone—it's not just alcoholics and drug-addicts, for all of us are suffering from the "spiritual malady" that plagues the West. One could even argue that our entire civilization has been rendered "powerless over alcohol" in the

---

[1] Jung, *CW*, vol. 6, para. 374.
[2] *Alcoholics Anonymous*, foreword to the first edition.

same way Jung humbly admitted that he was powerless to help Jaime or Rowland. The fact that the Twelve Steps continue to inch closer to the mainstream and that many groups are now filled with young people says volumes about our shared longing to restore our religious connection, to quench "the spiritual thirst of our being for wholeness, expressed in medieval language: the union with God," as Jung wrote to Wilson in 1961.[3] Moreover, the widespread nature of the disease speaks to the ineptitude of our traditional religious organizations in filling such a spiritual void.

As in all myth, the Steps portray a psychological journey which includes the metamorphosis of both humans and gods alike, representative of each of us individually as we embark upon a similar quest that Jung took, to discover a *myth of expanding consciousness* for ourselves. Indeed, the mystery of what it means to be fully human courses through the Steps (as in ancient myth), but now cloaked in modern language and ritual. And while the manner in which the symbols are presented might make it harder for us to classify the Steps as strictly "myth," it does make Wilson's pragmatic program a highly effective instrument of spiritual transformation. And just like Mountain Lake and his myth, or the Ajumawi and theirs, most of us won't have to try very hard to find our own story expressed in the Twelve Steps, or for them to infuse our lives with meaning, past, present, and future. Studying the Steps alongside Jung's method of individuation helps to uncover what makes them so effective, for the Steps fulfill the same religious function that the older myths once did, but

---

[3] Jung, *Letters*, vol. 2, pp. 623-25.

with one very important change: The characters that inhabited the central role in the ancient stories have been replaced by a nameless protagonist, whom I call "the Anonymous Alcoholic," a relatable participant in "the divine drama in which man plays"[4] in today's world.

God Is Dead

Fundamentally, the West has undergone a profound shift in our relationship to our religious myths; "an impoverishment of symbolism"[5] has left a gaping hole in our collective consciousness that is now being at least partially filled by a spiritual co-op of reformed drunks and drug addicts. A shift in perspective like the one that has befallen our religious symbols shouldn't come as a surprise though, for it has been oft decried since Nietzsche famously pointed it out in 1882, "God is dead." The dire need for a reformulation of our mythological lodestars has been expressed by many of recent history's most important thinkers, but the notion of an impending religious renaissance was perhaps most poignantly echoed (as recently as 1994) by the late Jungian author and analyst Edward Edinger. When asked whether Jung's method of individuation itself might ever fulfill the role as a new religious myth for the modern West, Edinger responded:

> It is perfectly clear that Jungian psychology as we know it, the individuation process—

---

[4] Jung, *CW*, vol. 11, para. 226.
[5] C. G. Jung, *Collected Works of C.G. Jung, Volume 9 (Part 1)*, ed. R. F.C. Hull (Princeton University Press, 2014), para. 50. Hereafter Jung, *CW*, vol. 9.

that laborious process that takes years of the analytic endeavor for each individual—is not going to be a very wide spread event. What I expect to happen will be that some collective phenomenon will emerge out of Jungian psychology that will speak to the unconscious of the masses directly. ... I anticipate that some kind of new mythological drama will derive from Jung's insights presumably generated by someone with a religious genius. ... And if that were to happen, then a new religion would be generated that allowed the masses to affirm instinctively (as doctrines rather than [intuited] facts) the basic points of individuation. That's my guess about how [a new myth] might unfold.[6]

As we've seen in previous chapters, the Steps did not emerge directly from Jungian psychology but are a phenomenon that grew alongside it, sprouting out of the same unconscious rhizome from which Jung's personal myth arose. In the chapters that follow, as we flesh out some of the basic points of individuation, we'll see how the Twelve Steps lead us in the same general direction as Jung's process—ever inward, where we finally discover what invigorates the human soul and inspires spiritual transformation. Such a study will necessitate

---

[6] From a talk called *Gnosticism and Early Christianity,* delivered by Edward Edinger at the C.G. Jung Institute in Los Angeles in 1994, reprinted with permission.

a close examination of the inherent darkness in the human psyche, elucidated by the pervasive psychospiritual illness of alcoholism and addiction—a rather common neurosis that stems directly from our collective shadow complex in response to our culture's loss of mythic connection.[7]

In making the case that Edinger's "prophecy" is being at least partially fulfilled in Wilson's Twelve Steps, the coming chapters will show how a working knowledge of Twelve Step principles can help one to understand the nature of psychological transformation in general, doing so through a classical Jungian lens. One thing promises to become clear: Wilson and Jung shared an intuitive religious sense that allowed them to channel the wisdom of the collective unconscious, resulting in striking similarities. Thus, we do both of them a great disservice by neglecting to thoughtfully compare and contrast their ideas regarding religious conversion, especially considering that in today's world so many who don't know where to find anything of real meaning and value have desperately turned to drugs and alcohol in an attempt to fill what we in fellowships have aptly named a "God-shaped hole."

---

[7] A "complex" in Jungian thought is a universal pattern of experience or behavior that is compulsive by nature. Complexes can be understood as being "autonomous" aspects of the psyche and can serve either "positive" or "negative" purposes.

6

The New God-Image

The nature of what we can expect to discover in our examination of the Steps is purely psychological. Wilson intuited early on that his own recovery hinged upon an improved conscious contact with a higher power of his own conception, and he would go on to formulate a psychological procedure designed to bring about just that. Jung had learned from William James that psychological development is intrinsically spiritual, explaining that "religious statements without exception have to do with the reality of the psyche and not with the reality of physis."[1] The word *psyche* in Greek means "soul," and for our purposes, the two are interchangeable—whatever is *spiritual* is inherently *psychological*, and vice-versa. Jung discovered he could use religious symbols as a means to examine the inner workings of the psyche, and coupled with the psychological nature of the Twelve Steps, his finding suggests that the less adorned a religious statement is by symbolical language, the more purely psychological it will be. That's why, despite its lack of

---

[1] Jung, *CW*, vol. 11, para. 751.

symbolical imagery, the Twelve Steps still represents a highly effective religious statement.[2]

For a spiritual process to be truly transformational, it must lead directly inward, into the realm of *Psyche*, beckoning us to examine the hidden psychological factors that brought us to this moment in time. *Psyche* represents the inner world where we uncover our compulsions and discover our vocation, a notion Jung borrowed from Paul indicative of the energizing function of spiritual transformation.[3] *Physis*, on the other hand, studies "the principle of growth or change in nature,"[4] accounting for all the "outside stuff" we secretly hope will make us feel complete, such as more money, a new partner

---

[2] Wilson's symbol for A.A. of a triangle within a circle, accompanied with the words Unity, Service, and Recovery inscribed along the edges of the triangle, is highly correlated to the mandalas that Jung noticed emerging spontaneously in the drawings of some of his patients who he felt had attained a degree of wholeness. Moreover, the circle and triangle is related to Jung's commentary on the alchemical idea of "squaring the circle." The following image, from Jung, *CW*, vol. 12, p. 125, is related to Wilson's circle and triangle, also pictured below:

[3] Regarding vocation, Jung writes: it is "an irrational factor [that] acts like a law of God from which there is no escape … as if it were a daemon whispering to him of new and wonderful paths. Anyone with a vocation hears the voice of the inner man: he is called." (Jung, *CW*, vol. 17, para. 300).
[4] Collins English Dictionary, s.v. "physis," April 12, 2023, https://www.collinsdictionary.com/us/dictionary/english/physis.

or a bigger house—things that have little impact on our continued spiritual well-being. Fundamentally, such a process is meant to aim the light of our expanding consciousness ever deeper into the dark crannies of the soul, initiating a shift in our attitude and perspective which remarkably leads to a shift in our behaviors. After that, we can expect a fundamental change in the "outside world" as well.

Wilson knew that lasting transformation hinges on a change in psyche first, that life's circumstances have little to do with one's ability to have a transformative experience: "When the spiritual malady is overcome, then we straighten out mentally and physically,"[5] he wrote. That is because "the main problem of the alcoholic centers in [the] mind."[6] Wilson had learned as much from Dr. Silkworth back at Towns, who concluded from his own research in treating upwards of 40,000 alcoholics that in addition to the physical condition the alcoholic suffers from, which the doctor dubbed "the phenomenon of craving," there is a mental component that must also be overcome: "Until [the alcoholic] is able to experience an entire psychic change, there is little hope of his [or her] recovery."[7] The same psychological factors that drive us to become powerless are what makes our lives unmanageable,

---

[5] *Alcoholics Anonymous*, 64.

[6] *Alcoholics Anonymous*, 23.

[7] *Alcoholics Anonymous*, xxviii. Silkworth had been relying on "moral psychology" to bring about such a change, and was well aware that certain types of alcoholics didn't respond to that kind of treatment, but was hesitant to prescribe spirituality. Once he saw the success that AA was having, he came around on the spiritual idea and even contributed a chapter to the book, called "The Doctor's Opinion," which was included as the preface.

and must be countered by a psychological process that Wilson ultimately referred to as "a spiritual awakening." The "entire psychic change" involves a fundamental shift that takes place in the baseline of our individual consciousness, illustrated in the powerful prescription that Jung gave to Rowland when he explained that "the vital spiritual experience" required to treat alcoholism is marked by "huge emotional displacements and rearrangements. Ideas, emotions, and attitudes which were once the guiding forces ... are suddenly cast to one side, and a completely new set of conceptions and motives begin to dominate."[8] Thus, our individual psychology forms the basis of our spiritual development, top to bottom, inside and out.

Jung's Psychological Approach

Such a mysterious metamorphosis is best described in myth, the ancient form of story-telling composed of paradoxical images reflective of the hidden dynamics and structure of the psyche. Recall that Jung's own myth was founded upon his approaching the symbols of the Taos legend from a psychological angle and extrapolating the universal truths therein. Throughout his career, Jung interpreted ancient myths through a similar lens in an attempt to shed as much light as he could on the inner workings of the human mind. And while Jung made clear that such insights may be gleaned from the myths of many different cultures, he was also acutely aware that in our modern era, religious statements are difficult to view symbolically, due to the illogical literalism foisted upon them:

---

[8] *Alcoholics Anonymous*, 27.

One cannot turn the clock back and force oneself to believe "what one knows is not true." But one could give a little thought to what the symbols really mean. In this way would not only the incomparable treasures of our civilization be conserved, but we should also gain new access to the old truths which have vanished from our "rational" purview because of the strangeness of their symbolism. How can a man be God's son and be born of a virgin? That is a slap in the face of reason. Today such dogmas fall on deaf ears, because nothing in our known world responds to such assertions. But if we understand these things for what they are, as symbols, then we can only marvel at the unfathomable wisdom that is in them and be grateful to the institution which has not only conserved them, but developed them dogmatically. The man of today lacks the very understanding that would help him to believe...

As a metaphysical "truth" [religious symbols] remained wholly inaccessible to me, and I suspect that I am by no means the only one to find himself in that position.[9]

What Jung proposes is a shift from the rationalism that separates us from our religious imagery and prevents us from relating to the symbols from a more personal, subjective point

_____
[9] Jung, *CW*, vol. 11, para. 294.

of view, what he called *the psychological approach*. Jung's experience with the Taos myth provides just one example of how he dealt with mythological symbols from *all* cultures— even those from his own Western background. Rather than "forcing himself to believe" that the legendary stories of ancient myths are true from a literal or historical standpoint, Jung chose to view them as emblematic of truth reflected in the human soul. Thankfully, to accept a religious myth as "psychologically true" does not mean that one must adopt religious teachings or dogma. Rather, one draws out personal meaning from the symbols directly, recognizing one's own journey into the psychic depths reflected therein—exactly what is conveyed in the Twelve Steps.

Such a change in perspective is key to unlocking a deeper understanding of our own spiritual quest, and it sits in sharp contrast to the commonly held practice handed down by generations of conventional religion that Jung called *the metaphysical approach*, which holds that religious symbols are concrete objects and/or historical facts, and that as such they should be taken at face value. As Westerners, the metaphysical approach is the one our minds are pre-programmed to run, whether we "believe in" religious dogma or not; it is our doctrinal "code," so to speak, and for many of us our spiritual "operating system is frozen," stuck trying to load the metaphysical approach and currently unable to accept any new input. Such a perspective is our greatest hindrance to our progression into the realm of the psyche, even if we are staunch non-believers of any particular faith, because it dims the useful lampposts that might have otherwise lit the path inward by reflecting upon the ancient imagery as a dynamic inherent within.

Wilson's (Psychological) Approach

Wilson learned from working with so many newcomers that his alcoholic readers would be similarly jaded by religious dogma, writing an entire chapter called "We Agnostics." In it, he begs us to "discard old ideas"[10] we have about spirituality and religion and to adopt an approach towards such concepts from a perspective comparable to Jung's: "Do not let any prejudice you have deter you from honestly asking yourself what [spiritual terms] mean to you. At the start, this was all we needed to commence spiritual growth, to effect our first conscious relation with God as we understood him."[11] Throughout the Big Book, Wilson demonstrates how easily one may pivot from the metaphysical approach; in the first chapter, "Bill's Story," he shares how he came upon his own unique psychological perspective, beginning with the most fundamental symbol of Western myth—what Jung called *the God-image*. Wilson tells us that when Ebby came to visit in Towns Hospital, he shared about the religious method he had been introduced to by Rowland Hazard and the Oxford Group. Listening to Ebby's newfound religious convictions, Wilson felt that he "couldn't believe in the God Ebby had talked about."[12] He understood Ebby's notion of God to be of the metaphysical variety—a variation of the same conception of the deity that all Westerners are born with. Bill describes his reluctance thusly:

---

[10] *Alcoholics Anonymous*, 52.
[11] *Alcoholics Anonymous*, 47.
[12] *Pass it On*, 120.

The word God still aroused a certain antipathy. When the thought was expressed that there might be a God personal to me this feeling was intensified. I didn't like the idea. I could go for such conceptions as Creative Intelligence, Universal Mind or Spirit of Nature but I resisted the thought of a Czar of the Heavens, however loving His sway might be. I have since talked with scores of men who felt the same way.[13]

Hearing Wilson's misgivings, Ebby could not have given a more inspired response, setting off the sea-change in Wilson's own religious attitude that sparked the formation of the most robust spiritual movement of the modern era: "Why don't you choose your own conception of God?" Wilson went on to share his epiphany spurred by Ebby's insightful question:

That statement hit me hard. It melted the icy intellectual mountain in whose shadow I had lived and shivered many years. I stood in the sunlight at last.

It was only a matter of being willing to believe in a Power greater than myself. Nothing more was required of me to make my beginning. I saw that growth could start from that point. Upon a foundation of complete willingness I might build what I saw in my friend. Would I have it? Of course I would!

---

[13] *Alcoholics Anonymous,* 12.

> Thus was I convinced that God is
> concerned with us humans when we want Him
> enough. At long last I saw, I felt, I believed.
> Scales of pride and prejudice fell from my eyes.
> A new world came into view.[14]

Like many, Wilson's journey toward a spiritual awakening began with his reconciliation with the God-image; his myth provides a template for those of the agnostic ilk who struggle to connect to traditional Western symbolism, who must also shift their perspective to a psychological one if they are to seize upon the transformational energy available through such symbols. Demonstrated time and again in the fellowships is just how effective such change in perspective can be; in Wilson's case, the moment he sincerely considered the unorthodox approach Ebby suggested, allowing his own God-image to morph into a psychological construct, he was catapulted into a new way of perceiving the world, what he called "the fourth dimension of existence":[15] "There was a sense of victory, followed by such a peace and serenity as I had never known. There was utter confidence. I felt lifted up, as though the great clean wind of a mountain top blew through and through. God comes to most men gradually, but His impact

---

[14] *Alcoholics Anonymous*, 12. William Schaberg, in *Writing the Big Book*, proposes that Wilson's representation of this conversation with Thacher, found in "Bill's Story," is perhaps the most egregious example of his penchant for "mythmaking," pointing out that there are no contemporary historical documents to support that such a conversation ever took place between Wilson and Thacher. Moreover, Schaberg tells us that Thacher admitted on multiple occasions that he does not recall having said it.
[15] *Alcoholics Anonymous*, 25.

on me was sudden and profound."[16] The entire Twelve Step movement grew out of Wilson's acceptance of a psychological interpretation of the God-image, for he quickly realized that there were "thousands of alcoholics who might gladly have what had been so freely given to [him]"[17]— "a God we can do business with," as we often hear in meetings. Since then, recovery culture has become saturated with a God-concept similar to the one Wilson (and Jung) discovered, suggesting that the road to recovery doesn't begin when one decides to quit drinking at all, but rather with one's decision to reconceive the symbol of God for oneself. Once that fundamental psychic change occurs, it opens the door to a cascade of "emotional displacements and rearrangements" that Jung promised Rowland would follow. The simplicity of Ebby's response to Bill represents perhaps the most distinguishing aspect of Twelve Step spirituality, its ability to fundamentally change the way Westerners access God's power.

An Immaculate Conception

This ground-breaking idea (for the modern West) would be carefully built upon by Wilson and friends in the early days of AA, cementing a psychological framework for understanding the God-image from its very beginning. What naturally unfolded from Ebby's invitation for Wilson to choose his own conception of God was the statement that was practically stapled onto Steps Three and Eleven: "God as we understood

---

[16] *Alcoholics Anonymous*, 14.
[17] *Alcoholics Anonymous*, 14.

Him." In the Twelve Step fellowships, each member believes that every other member's conception of God is as viable as their own in bringing to pass individual transformation— regardless of who or what that conception is. One might even hear an old-timer gently reassure a newcomer struggling to develop a personal relationship with a higher power: "Do you believe that I believe? If so, then you can use my Higher Power until you find one for yourself. In the meantime, make a list of all the attributes you want your God to have, then start asking it to keep you sober each day, and we'll see what happens." After only a few weeks or months, that same person, who formerly struggled with practically every aspect of life, will have found a God they can trust and began to transform their lives from the inside out.

In many ways the God of the Twelve Steps is identical to the "subjectively conditioned"[18] God that Jung pursued throughout his career, of which there is neither question nor debate about whether or not it is "real" or whose conception of it is the "one true one." In fact, the nature of the God-image is almost never discussed in Twelve Step meetings; participants understand that "the word *God* is just a placeholder," that the particular God-concept of any individual member is not important, that each may believe in their own way and still effect a viable relationship with whatever God they choose. Thus, the fluidity of the God-image as a symbol, rather than its dogmatic fixedness, is paramount in the Twelve Step

---

[18] Jung said, "I cannot but regard all assertions about God as relative because subjectively conditioned." Jung, *Letters*, vol. 2, p. 368. William James called such a conception "pluralistic."

fellowships, even for those members who still believe in a more conventional conception. One anonymous member often shares a profound truth that seems to have been long lost upon much of the West: "In our fellowship, even God is anonymous." In a similar sentiment, Jung said that "God has one thousand names,"[19] and if Twelve Step experience has taught us anything, it is that those 1,000 names have 10,000 different meanings. Wilson thus urges his readers to consider "a God of their own understanding" as they follow him down the trail of self-searching and self-discovery, for the power we need to recreate our lives can only be found buried beneath our longest-held religious preconceptions.

---

[19] C.G. Jung, *Collected Works of C.G. Jung, Volume 9 (Part 2): Aion: Researches into the Phenomenology of the Self*, ed. R. F.C. Hull, vol. 9ii (Princeton University Press, 2014), par. 182.

7

The Great Reality

Learning to decode the language of myth is vital to unlocking the power embedded within its images—no easy task, even when the symbolism has been whittled down to the bare bones of a fundamental psychological process, as it has been in the Twelve Steps. Joseph Campbell, the popular author and lecturer of mythological and religious themes and contemporary of Jung and Wilson, offers his perspective on how the metaphysical approach has inadvertently blocked our access to the power of religious symbolism:

> [Symbols are the] catalysts of the numinous—
> and therein lies the secret of their force.
> However, the traits of symbols and elements
> of myths tend to acquire a power of their own
> through association, by which access of the
> numinous itself may become blocked. And it
> does, indeed, become blocked when the images
> are insisted upon as final terms in themselves:
> as they are, for example, in a dogmatic credo.[1]

---

[1] Joseph Campbell, *The Masks of God: Oriental Mythology* (Novato, California: New World Library, 2021), p. 45.

Campbell's way of thinking is especially relevant regarding our new approach to the Western God-image: Within the context of certain religious dogmas, *the Czar of Heaven* represents an objective statement of fact, what Campbell calls "a final term," and a known stranger to the human psyche. Conversely, the arguably more inspiring (and sophisticated) approach to the God-image is *purely* psychological, interpreting that fundamental symbol as evocative of our longing for deeper connection to each other and to the Universe, as well as the power that makes such connections possible. Jung explained: "'God' is a primordial experience of man, and from the remotest times humanity has taken inconceivable pains either to portray this baffling experience, to assimilate it by means of interpretation, speculation, and dogma, or else to deny it."[2] And while the symbol of God is meant to evoke such a "primordial experience," its power to do so becomes blurred when we hold it to be a somatic being somewhere else other than right here and now, in the soul of humankind, where and when we need it most.

The Psychological Function of the God-image

Edward Edinger, the prolific Jungian author, demonstrates that the word "symbol" is itself illustrative of our sense of separation from the God-image and our longing to reconnect with it, what Jung called our "spiritual thirst for wholeness." Examining its etymology, Edinger explains that religious imagery is reflective of the notion that, psychologically speaking, we have been cut

---

[2] Jung, *CW*, vol. 11, para. 480.

off from a part of ourselves that we now unconsciously long to be restored to:

> The word symbol derives from the Greek word *symbolon* which combines two root words, *sym*, meaning together or with, and *bolon*, meaning that which has been thrown. The basic meaning is thus "that which has been thrown together." In original Greek usage, symbols referred to the two halves of an object such as a stick or a coin which two parties broke between them as a pledge and to prove later the identity of the presenter of one part to the holder of the other. The term corresponded to our word tally concerning which Webster's unabridged dictionary states: "It was customary for traders, after notching a stick to show the number or quantity of goods delivered, to split it lengthwise through the notches so that the parts exactly corresponded, the seller keeping one stick, and the purchaser the other. A symbol was thus originally a tally referring to the missing piece of an object which when restored to, or thrown together with, its partner recreated the original whole object." This corresponds to our understanding of the psychological function of a symbol. The symbol leads us to the missing part of the whole man. It relates us to our original totality. It heals our split, our alienation from life. And since the

whole man is a great deal more than the ego,
[the symbol] relates us to the supra-personal
forces which are the source of our being and
our meaning. This is the reason for honoring
subjectivity and cultivating the symbolic life.[3]

Edinger, like Wilson and Jung, urges us to consider religious symbols as a means to restore our connection to the spiritual forces within us, but from which we believe we have been split off. "The psychological function of a symbol" is significant as we begin the internal pilgrimage, for right where we honestly encounter our own conception of the God-image is where we *also* confront our brokenness, or the core belief that each of us holds that we are undeserving and/or unlovable, reflected in the very old and entrenched dogma which states that since the Fall of Adam and Eve, few (if any) individuals have been worthy enough to have their relationship with deity restored in this life.

And while religious symbols are meant to heal that primordial split in the psyche, as we learn when we take the Steps, we can't be made whole until we become conscious of the fact that at some point, we were separated from that which we now (unconsciously) long for. However, uncovering the evidence of such a split isn't so easy; even those of us who suffer from the level of delusion that defines alcoholism or addiction have a hard time coming to terms with the glaring

---

[3] Edward F. Edinger, *Ego and Archetype: Individuation and the Religious Function of the Psyche,* (Boulder, Colorado: Shambhala, 2017), p. 130. Hereafter, *Ego and Archetype*.

truth about it. Ironically, we find the proof of what is missing scattered among the broken pieces of our lives: Our need for spiritual help is only ever exposed through a psychic fracture that befalls us at the very moment all hope is lost—"when there is no friendly direction," as the late Clancy I., perhaps the most renowned AA speaker often said. That's why "hitting bottom" turns out to be our greatest blessing, for it ushers in an attitude best described by the Twelve Step acronym, "G.O.D., the gift of desperation." Indeed, one of the great paradoxes of the journey toward authentic spirituality is that it sprouts out of the very moment we feel the most alienated from our Source. Before we are led back to the missing parts of ourselves, as Edinger suggested, before we can be made whole through the power discovered in the religious imagery presented in Steps Two and Three, we must accept the harsh reality implied by Step One. Thankfully, by the time we "fully [conceded] to our innermost selves that we were alcoholic,"[4] we had already made huge strides toward cultivating the type of self-searching required for a restoration to take place.

The Real Problem with Western Metaphysics

Interestingly, our ability to accept our brokenness is intricately tied to the way in which we conceive of the God-image, so adopting a psychological approach is very important to our quest for enlightenment. Even though each of us carries an innate God-image, as Campbell says, we are cut off from its *numinosity* (its restorative power) inasmuch as we project it

---

[4] *Alcoholics Anonymous*, 30.

out into the universe, a pervasive condition resulting from the metaphysical approach having beguiled the West for many centuries now. To entertain an extroverted conception of the God-image is to be prohibited from accessing its transformative power because such a perspective makes it almost impossible for one to take accountability for one's life. Said another way, *one cannot see oneself objectively until one recognizes the subjective nature of one's own religious beliefs*—whether one is atheist, agnostic, or a staunch believer. Jung describes this strange psychological feedback loop thusly:

> An exclusively religious projection may rob the soul of its values so that through sheer inanition it becomes incapable of further development and gets stuck in an unconscious state. At the same time they fall victim to the delusion that the cause of all misfortune lies outside, and people no longer stop to ask themselves how far it is their doing. If the soul no longer has any part to play, religious life congeals into externals and formalities. ... It may easily happen, therefore, that a Christian who believes in all the sacred figures is still undeveloped and unchanged in his inmost soul because he has "all God outside" and does not experience him in the soul. His deciding motives, his ruling interests and impulses, do not spring from the sphere of Christianity but from the unconscious and undeveloped psyche, which is as pagan and archaic as ever.

> Not the individual alone but the sum total of
> individuals living in a nation proves the truth of
> this contention.[5]

Jung learned early on from watching his own father, a devout pastor of the Swiss Reformed Church, that it is not uncommon for a person to "believe in" all of the externalized images of a particular religion and yet remain fundamentally undeveloped and unchanged inwardly. On the other hand, the more open-minded we are regarding our spiritual beliefs, the more capable we will become in seeing the truth about ourselves, whereas an "all-outside" God-concept makes the already difficult task of spiritual growth all but impossible, for it cuts off one's access to the symbol's numinosity. A religious attitude which "fancies God as an external object of worship" mirrors the delusion that each of us suffers from time to time that something or someone outside of ourselves has the power to fix us—perhaps the most glaring symptom of spiritual malady.[6]

The Objective Psyche

The God-image is emblematic of many things, not the least of which is the conjunction of the aspects of our nature

---

[5] C. G. Jung, *Collected Works of C.G. Jung, Volume 12: Psychology and Alchemy*, ed. R. F.C. Hull (Princeton University Press, 2014), para. 11.
[6] James Hollis, Jungian Author and Analyst, adds: "If we are not experiencing divinity within us in some way, it will come to possess us, through our projection of it onto the outer world. Or go inward unconsciously and emerge as symptoms." James Hollis, *Through the Dark Wood: Finding Meaning in the Second Half of Life*, (Boulder, CO: Sounds True, 2014), audiobook, 6:23.

which are fundamentally at odds with each other—the side of us that longs for a restoration—and the other that hinders such—our feelings of inadequacy fueled by resentment, fear, and shame. Since those of us who have been forced into a spiritual dilemma, such as alcoholism or addiction, can no longer hide from the truth about the cause of our misfortunes, ironically, we are *also* fated to be brought face to face with our conception of the God-image. Thankfully, Wilson developed a process in the Big Book that methodically (and safely) guides his readers on how to "make the approach":[7]

> Deep down in every man, woman, and child, is the fundamental idea of God. It may be obscured by calamity, by pomp, by worship of other things, but in some form or other it is there. For faith in a Power greater than ourselves, and miraculous demonstrations of that power in human lives, are facts as old as man himself.
>
> We finally saw that faith in some kind of God was a part of our make-up, just as much as the feeling we have for a friend. Sometimes we had to search fearlessly, but He was there. He was as much a fact as we were. We found the Great Reality deep down within us. In the last analysis it is only there that He may be found. It was so with us. We can only clear the ground a bit. If our testimony helps sweep

---

[7] *Alcoholics Anonymous*, 46.

> away prejudice, enables you to think honestly, encourages you to search diligently within yourself, then, if you wish, you can join us on the Broad Highway. With this attitude you cannot fail. The consciousness of your belief is sure to come to you.[8]

Having worked with scores of newcomers to the fledgling fellowship, by the time he wrote the Big Book, Bill recognized that it is nearly impossible for most people to believe that anything good exists within, let alone the omnipotent God. But his intuition allowed him to sense, like Jung, that the God-image is in fact an aspect of our very being, a baseline component deep in the unconscious psyche of every man, woman, and child. And yet, if God really does dwell in the human soul, it's a place most of us wouldn't dare to look, even if we knew how. Turning inward is usually our last resort, but doing so paves the way to seeing who we really are, to discovering "the Great Reality"—what Jung called the *objective psyche*, another term for his notion of the collective unconscious.

Here, Wilson's myth underscores the antidote to the spiritual condition that now plagues a culture defined by materialism—the belief that everything good lies outside—by replacing the image of *the Czar of Heaven* with a psychologically based concept, Wilson opened himself up to the recognition that his "troubles were of [his] own making, that they arose out of [him]self."[9] The more we align ourselves with the

---

[8] *Alcoholics Anonymous*, 55.
[9] *Alcoholics Anonymous*, 62.

notion of God as a subjective *power* (as suggested in Steps Two and Three), the more empowered we become in the fearless and searching self-appraisal suggested in Steps Four through Ten. Thus, by addressing our natural tendency as Westerners to view the God-image as "a final term," the Twelve Step myth engenders within us the wherewithal to solve many of our own problems, for by accepting ourselves as the root cause of our troubles, we quit looking outside of ourselves for something to fix us, including our notion of the God-image.

Typically, ministers of Western religion reject the idea that the Great Reality can *only* be found in the dark recesses of each individual's psyche; yet, from the psychological perspective, the extroverted style of worship many of them preach is far more heretical, being perhaps one reason why so many have so much difficulty taking accountability for their lives. Thus, Jung wrote, in all earnestness: "It would be blasphemy to assert that God can manifest himself everywhere save only in the human soul." Nonetheless, the implications of such a close arrangement between us and our gods is hard to fathom, especially if we are still entrapped by Western metaphysics. Jung goes on to explain why it is that we should endeavor to adopt a psychological approach, drawing kickback from the ministry, many of whom vehemently condemned him throughout his career: "To carry a god around in yourself means a great deal," he writes, "it is a guarantee of happiness, of power, and even of omnipotence, insofar as these are attributes of divinity. To carry a god within oneself is practically the same as being God oneself."[10]

---

[10] Jung, *CW*, vol. 12, para. 11.

Thus, Jung insisted that digging through the dank soil of our own psychology for the truth about ourselves is our greatest responsibility and that avoidance of such a task, now an unwanted byproduct of being born into Western culture, produces nothing more than a shell of a human who lacks awareness of their most glaring faults, incapable of grasping the Great Reality. Sadly, by insisting that God is "a final term," conventional religion feeds into the delusion that we are not the cause of our troubles, thereby blocking us from any real solutions, spiritual and otherwise. But the Twelve Steps counter this tendency by guiding us to take full accountability for our behaviors and our lives while at the same time instructing us on how to author our own religious beliefs—the essence of viewing oneself from the perspective of the Great Reality. By earnestly reckoning with the God-image, which naturally leads to the adoption of a psychological approach, we counter our innate reluctance to search everywhere but inside of ourselves for anything of real meaning and value.

8

The Breath of Life

The way Jung approached religious symbolism was informed by both his scientific background as well as the intuitions he garnered through his own plunge into the unconscious. By isolating symbolical elements embedded in the dreams of his patients and comparing them to those within a wide array of ancient narratives, Jung found that certain images are repeated, spanning cultural and religious landscapes from every corner of the world and throughout all of human history. He postulated that deep in the unconscious, we are all connected by way of these fundamental, shared images, and he called them *archetypes of the collective unconscious*, reasoning that some mythical images are so intrinsic to the human psyche that they form the very basis of consciousness— perhaps his greatest contribution to the field of science.

Jung's findings had enormous impact, though he recognized that he was by no means the first to take up such a perspective:

> All ages before us have believed in gods in some form or other. Only an unparalleled impoverishment of symbolism could enable

> us to rediscover the gods as psychic factors,
> that is, as archetypes of the unconscious. . .
> Heaven has become for us the cosmic space
> of the physicists, and the divine empyrean a
> fair memory of things that once were. But "the
> heart glows," and a secret unrest gnaws at the
> roots of our being.[1]

And while James, Jung, Campbell, Edinger, and a few other 20th-century thinkers, influenced by modern science, wrote about the psychological nature of the gods and the God-image, Wilson and the newly sober cohorts of the "alcoholic squad" of the Oxford Group, as early as 1934, had found a way to treat alcoholism utilizing a similar approach. Yet, as we'll see in the next few chapters, its roots predate the late 19th- and early 20th-century visionaries; in the West, there were a few medieval Christian mystics who had first employed something akin to a psychological perspective, prompting Jung to admit that in modern times we have only *re*discovered the gods as such.

Meister Eckhart

Jung's way of thinking about God and spirituality was deeply influenced by the writings of one ancient in particular, an obscure Christian mystic named Meister Eckhart, a forward-thinking Dominican theologian from the 13th century. Jung began studying Eckhart when he was only 15 years old, and he once remarked that of all the ancients he read, he identified

---

[1] Jung, *CW*, vol. 9i, para. 50.

with Eckhart the most, having discovered in him "the breath of life."[2] As a teenager, during their many "heated theological debates,"[3] the introverted style of worship that Jung learned from the Dominican stood in sharp contrast to his father's conventional attitude, contributing to his later differentiation of the psychological approach from that of traditional metaphysics. In his book *Psychological Types*, Jung included an essay in which he breaks down the psychological perspective he saw in the writings of Eckhart, who believed that God is most readily discovered within the soul of fallen men and women. Eckhart reported his deep feeling of kinship with the Divine with amazing clarity, in words that spoke deeply to the precocious young man: "The eye through which I see God is the same eye through which God sees me; my eye and God's eye are one eye, one seeing, one knowing, one love. … Man is truly God and God is truly man."[4] As a Christian mystic, Eckhart believed—like Wilson and Jung—that the gods are intrinsically connected to the human psyche. The term *mysticism* means "union with the absolute."

Beautiful as Eckhart's depictions were, what interests us here is Jung's analytical perspective on the mystic's religious approach, since that is what will tie our practice to the expansive spirituality that we share with each of them. First, we must understand how Eckhart's revolutionary writings, in his day considered heresy, impacted those who came after him. In *Doorways to the Self*, Steven Herrmann explores how instrumental Eckhart was in helping both William James and

---

[2] Cited in Herrmann, *Doorways*, 32,38.
[3] Herrmann, *Doorways*, 34.
[4] Cited in Jung, CW, vol. 6, paras. 418-420.

Carl Jung develop their unique conceptions of religious imagery, explaining that Eckhart is "the missing link ... between Jung and James."[5] Herrmann posits that "the basic attitude Jung found in William James and that so appealed to him when he rediscovered his soul [after meeting James in 1909 at Clark University] is a similar one he'd discovered first in adolescence when he studied Eckhart."[6] Addressing an audience of Jungian analysts, many of whom have also "rediscovered the gods as a psychic factor," Herrmann emphasizes the prescient nature of Eckhart's relationship to his higher power: "Eckhart was so far ahead of his time that he anticipated both James and Jung. Indeed, Eckhart anticipated where we all are today by 700 years!"[7] Having established that Wilson adopted a similar psychological approach as Jung toward the God-image, we can now begin to see how James, Jung, and Wilson inadvertently settled upon a similar religious attitude as the ancient mystic, one which we'll see aligns with Eastern and archaic forms as well.

As stated previously, in Eckhart's era, religious ideas like his were considered heretical and punishable by death, and he was tried by the church authorities, who accused him of "[leading] simple and uneducated people into error."[8] Thankfully, the seer passed away from natural causes during the months his tribunal was being held, skirting a certain violent and painful death. At that point most of his writings

---

[5] Herrmann, *Doorways*, 100, footnote 18.
[6] Herrmann, *Doorways*, 155.
[7] Herrmann, *Doorways*, 155.
[8] Meister Eckhart and Houston Smith, *Meister Eckhart: The Essential Sermons, Commentaries, Treatises and Defense*, trans. Edmund Colledge and Bernard McGinn, New edition (New York: Paulist Press, 1981), p. 10.

were destroyed, although some were stowed away, coming to light in the 19th century as Western philosophers (both within and without the Church) became interested in the mystical ideas he advanced. To this day Eckhart is considered an important theologian, having gained notoriety among those interested in drawing parallels between Christian mysticism and Eastern religious ideology, a school of Western thought largely pioneered by William James and carried forth by Jung, who wrote in *Psychological Types*:

> Strangely appealing is Eckhart's sense of an inner affinity with God, when contrasted with the [Western] sense of sin. We feel ourselves transported back into the spacious atmosphere of the Upanishads. Eckhart must have experienced a quite extraordinary enhancement of the value of the soul, i.e., of his own inner being, that enabled him to rise to a purely psychological and relativistic conception of God and of his relation to man. This discovery and painstaking exposition of the relativity of God to man and the soul seem to me one of the most important landmarks on the way to a psychological understanding of religious phenomena, serving at the same time to liberate the religious function from the cramping limitations of intellectual criticism, though this criticism, of course, must not be denied its dues.[9]

---

[9] Jung, CW, vol. 6, para. 411.

Here we see echoes of Wilson's approach come through in Jung's assessment of Eckhart. The ancient mystic could already sense the emergence of the spiritual malady forming in Western consciousness even back then, and it inspired him to search within just as it has done for us. Jung says that Eckhart's conception of God was "relativistic," growing out of a careful examination of his own inner being, further highlighting the subjective nature of every *myth of expanding consciousness*. Ironically, it was Wilson's underscoring of the subjectivity of his own conception of the God-image that made it suffice: "Our own conception, however inadequate, was enough to make the approach."[10] As we explored in the last chapter, in the Twelve Steps, "the relativity of God" is the cornerstone upon which our spiritual structure is built, the very thing that empowers us to see ourselves and the world around us through the eyes of the Great Reality.

An Inadequate Conception

Tucked in his commentary regarding Eckhart, Jung explains that to access the numinosity of the religious archetype, we must recognize it as a subjective construct and that we can't arrive at such a perspective until we quit "fetching God from without:"[11]

> [The relativity of God] implies a reciprocal
> and essential relation between man and God,

---

[10] *Alcoholics Anonymous*, 46.
[11] Jung, *CW*, vol. 6, para. 417.

whereby man can be understood as a function of God, and God as a psychological function of man... From the metaphysical point of view God is, of course, absolute, existing in himself. This implies his complete detachment from the unconscious, which means, psychologically, a complete unawareness of the fact that God's action springs from one's own inner being. The relativity of God, on the other hand, means that a not inconsiderable portion of the unconscious processes is registered, at least indirectly, as a psychological content. Naturally this insight is possible only when more attention than usual is paid to the psyche.[12]

Ironically, a conventional approach not only blocks us from recognizing that our troubles are of our own making, but it also prohibits us from recognizing our own divinity, as Jung explains in the foregoing quote. Thus, to become aware that the power of God emanates from a hidden source deep within the psyche requires first that we pierce through our metaphysical preconceptions about the God-image, an attitude which (unfortunately) does not come about without a considerable amount of psychological pain—sine qua non for an encounter with the numinosum. Wilson was inclined to register his experience of the Absolute as a function of the psyche as well, writing two years after the Big Book was published that he had

---

[12] Jung, *CW*, vol. 6, para. 412.

"tapped an unsuspected inner resource,"[13] similar to what Jung called "the transcendent function"[14] of the psyche. And while we note that such a "God-consciousness"[15] constitutes a relative psychological construct, it is the very thing that makes it sufficient to change us nonetheless, having "absolute ascendency over the will of the subject, and can therefore bring about or enforce actions and achievements that could never be done by conscious effort."[16]

Jung's postulate regarding a transcendent function concealed within the human mind is affirmed by Twelve Step experience, for our own "inadequate conception"[17] of God proved to be more effective than the almighty *Czar of Heaven* in getting us sober—tapping into an "unsuspected [i.e. unconscious] inner resource" was what finally empowered us to "accomplish those things ... which we could never do by ourselves."[18] Yet, it was a power we couldn't really plug into until we had learned to "get out of the way." To access the transcendent function of the psyche, Jung says that we have to make space for the Unconscious to reprogram and reboot our conscious mind from the inside out—to "let go and let God"—another mystical idea rooted in the psychological approach, a common thread running through the teachings of many of our spiritual ancestors, including Wilson, Jung, and Eckhart:

---

[13] *Alcoholics Anonymous*, 567.
[14] Jung, *CW*, vol. 6, para. 759.
[15] *Alcoholics Anonymous*, 568.
[16] Jung, *CW*, vol. 6, para. 412.
[17] *Alcoholics Anonymous*, 46.
[18] *Alcoholics Anonymous, 23.*

> The art of letting things happen, action through
> non-action, letting go of oneself as taught by
> Meister Eckhart, became for me [Jung] the
> key that opens the door to the way. We must
> be able to let things happen in the psyche …
> an art of which most people know nothing.
> Consciousness is forever interfering, helping,
> correcting, and negating, never leaving the
> psychic processes to grow in peace. It would be
> simple enough, if only simplicity were not the
> most difficult of all things.[19]

Being thus rooted in the psychological approach, the same
kinds of paradoxes we encounter in the writings of Eckhart
and Jung, such as the relativity of the God-image and action
through inaction, are familiar to us through our Twelve Step
practice. But they are impossible to grasp until we "let go
absolutely,"[20] as Wilson wrote, whose particular vocation
permitted him to make many such complex notions accessible
to us, the uninitiated in advanced philosophy, theology, or
psychology.

An Eastern Approach

And while Western religions have spent centuries concretizing
their various creeds and doctrines regarding the immutability
of the Absolute, what took place in the quiet recesses of the

---

[19] Jung, *CW*, vol. 13, para. 20.
[20] *Alcoholics Anonymous*, 58.

soul of an ancient mystic, when the God-image began to register as an aspect of his own interior being, was of historical theological importance: Jung comments that Eckhart's relativistic conception of God was "a landmark" on the way to a psychological understanding of religious phenomena, ultimately paving the way for each of us to "rediscover the gods as a psychic factor." And as Eckhart's philosophies reconnect us to our Western theosophical roots, they also show us where our modern spiritual practice resembles that of the ancient East. We got a glimpse of this when Jung pointed out that reading Eckhart "transports us back into the spacious atmosphere of the Upanishads." Our emerging notion of God as an inner resource, while distinct from the typical concretized Western God-image, is akin to a religious concept from the East known as Brahman, described by Jung as "the breath of life and the cosmic principle."[21]

Eastern religion is fundamentally introspective, distinct from the West's entrenched extroverted worship style. Today, the relativity of God is practiced "one day at a time" in Twelve Step groups around the world—by people who for the most part will probably never know how historically significant the advanced theology they've stumbled into really is. For, while both East and West ascribe cosmic power to their religious figures, the Western relationship to such energy is worlds apart. The many mythological images present in Eastern religion—resplendent with its own demons, dragons, and demigods—are understood by practitioners to be reflective of psychic energies, in sharp contrast to our own literalism

---

[21] Jung, *CW*, vol. 6, para. 334.

when we mistake the symbols for real-life, historical figures. Thus, many well-meaning Western agnostics, in their longing to forge a meaningful connection to myth, have ironically tried to adopt Eastern practices, never having been shown that an even more powerful, life-altering mystical experience is available to them if they would only try to view the religious imagery from their own culture with the same introverted attitude that their Eastern gurus teach—beginning with their very own God-image.

Jung implored Western agnostics to think carefully before trying to adopt Eastern (or primitive) forms of spirituality, warning against using it as yet another attempt to "avoid [one's] own dark corners."[22] While it is true that Eastern myth contains useful spiritual concepts, of even greater value to us would be risking an adventure inward, to see what kind of Cosmic connection we might discover by examining our own shadow and integrating our own demons. Until then, Jung warns that to try to adopt Eastern forms of spirituality only serves to distract the weary Westerner from the one thing that could actually "fix it":

> By an inevitable decree of fate the West is
> becoming acquainted with the peculiar facts of
> Eastern spirituality. It is useless either to belittle
> these facts, or to build false and treacherous
> bridges over yawning gaps. Instead of learning
> the spiritual techniques of the East by heart
> and imitating them in a thoroughly [Western]

------

[22] Jung, *CW*, vol. 11, para. 939.

way—*imitatio Christi!*—with a correspondingly forced attitude, it would be far more to the point to find out whether there exists in the unconscious an introverted tendency similar to that which has become the guiding spiritual principle of the East. We should then be in a position to build on our own ground with our own methods. If we snatch these things directly from the East, we have merely indulged our Western acquisitiveness, confirming yet again that "everything good is outside," whence it has to be fetched and pumped into our barren souls. It seems to me that we have really learned something from the East when we understand that the psyche contains riches enough without having to be primed from outside, and when we feel capable of evolving out of ourselves with or without divine grace. ... We must get at the Eastern values from within and not from without, seeking them in ourselves, in the unconscious.[23]

Because the Eastern religious attitude is psychological by nature, instead of trying to practice Eastern methods in our thoroughly Western way (the only way we know), we can seek out the same insights that draw us to the Eastern traditions within our own psyche. Wilson's is a perfect case in point that the psyche is primed for a fullness of spiritual experience,

---

[23] Jung, *CW*, Vol. 11, para. 10.

needing little outside influence from any religion, East or West, to activate. Wilson began his journey by adopting a relative perspective of the Western God-image, and that allowed him to build a bridge over the "yawning gap" that prevents Westerners from successfully practicing Eastern (or primitive) spirituality by itself. Wilson thus arrived at the same technique ("the guiding spiritual principles of the East") by searching for meaning and value within his own cultural context, showing us how to mine the gems we hope to discover from other cultures' religious traditions directly from within. Wilson's *myth of expanding consciousness*, though highly correlated with Eastern and primitive forms, emerged out of the ground of his own psyche, sparked by his earnest engagement with religious symbols with which he was already familiar. That, in turn, allowed him to address the fundamental needs of his Western point of view, including a reconciliation with the "all-outside" God-image as well as his need for individuality— offering further evidence that deep down, all humans are connected by way of our shared longing for psychological union with the Divine.

9

The Numinosum

Shaped Energy

The deeper we probe into the past in our examination of religious symbolism, the deeper we plunge into the collective unconscious. Highly fluid, relativized conceptions, such as Wilson's "God-consciousness" or Eckhart's "relative God-image" are related to conceptions of the divine from earliest times. Symbols like these elucidate certain truths about human psychology that are not readily apparent to our modern minds, evincing a fundamental dynamic that exists within the soul called *the numinosum*, the energy that comprises all religious archetypes and which generates the impetus within the psyche necessary for us to change.

In *Psychological Types*, Jung explores what lies beneath even the most ancient of religious images: "Symbols are shaped energies, determining ideas whose affective power is just as great as their spiritual value."[1] The "spiritual value" of a mythological symbol is what exists on the surface level of its narrative, the moral lesson entwined within the metaphysical dogma levied upon it, like Moses's Ten Commandments or

---

[1] Jung, *CW*, Vol. 6, para. 425.

the Beatitudes of Jesus. Such lessons have plenty of spiritual value, especially within the context of the society in which the associated myth has meaning. However, "the affective power" of a religious myth to transform the human psyche is not didactic at all, a lesson many of us in recovery had to learn the hard way: No matter how "good" we were, no matter how disciplined in obeying the rules, religious or otherwise, we still could not find the strength to quit. Bill highlights the nature of this terrible dilemma thusly: "If a mere code of morals or a better philosophy of life were sufficient to overcome alcoholism, many of us would have recovered long ago."[2] There is even a running joke among Twelve Step practitioners that we have been the boon of the self-help book industry, having tried everything we could think of to stop, including psychotherapy, baptism, holistic diets, exercise, exorcism, yoga, prayer and meditation, and every conceivable concoction of psychiatric medication known to humankind—every alcoholic and addict has their own extensive catalog of "methods we have tried," and as Wilson says, "could increase the list ad infinitum."[3] Yet, we finally had to surrender to the daunting fact that nothing would work, no matter how diligent we were or how badly we wanted it. In fact, even the Steps are not an end in themselves. Like every other religious symbol, they merely illuminate a path that leads inward, where we tap directly into the only solution to alcoholism and addiction the world has ever known, the "affective power" buried within our religious symbols. Jung, who understood well that sobriety is impossible

---

[2] *Alcoholics Anonymous*, 44.
[3] *Alcoholics Anonymous*, 31.

for a real alcoholic without an ongoing engagement with the numinosum, said it this way: "Behavior prescribed by rule is a substitute for spiritual transformation."[4] Knowing how badly Rowland needed "a vital spiritual experience," Jung urged him to go outside of the confines of conventional religion (and psychology) in search of it, which unfortunately may not have much to offer beyond a prescribed set of rules.

A religious symbol will "exert the formative influence natural to it"[5] as our conception of it begins to shift. The "formative influence" is the symbol's energetic attribute sparked by our interaction with it in an authentic, sincere way. And yet, that power exists within the human psyche regardless of its particular mythological framework—what Jung calls its "shape." Like the characters that present themselves to us in our nightly dreams, mythological symbols are shaped because they have been endowed with names, personalities, costumes, skin color, and so on. A symbol that has humanlike characteristics, such as the God-image, Mountain Lake's ancestors, or the Anonymous Alcoholic, is called an *anthropomorphic* symbol, while symbols with animallike traits such as the snake, the buffalo, or the coyote are *theriomorphic*. Not all religious symbols have agency, however, or even present themselves as living beings—sometimes they appear in the form of the sun, the moon, a rock, a river, a cross, a mandala, or any number of static shapes or protocols, such as the hero's journey into the unconscious or the psychic pilgrimage laid out in the Twelve Steps.

---

[4] Jung, *CW*, vol. 9, para. 243.
[5] Jung, *CW*, Vol. 12, para. 12.

What's required of us in order to activate the symbol's transformative power is not that we abandon our ingrained perception of it. Rather, when we rerelate ourselves to its shape, viewing it as an inner, psychic resource, its energy begins to manifest in our lives. Jung's remark that "symbols are shaped energies" holds the key to such an approach: When one looks beyond the outwardly projected God-image, the "shape" slinks back into the unconscious, and "[it] becomes an autonomous psychic complex."[6] At that point, the shape that the symbol previously embodied becomes irrelevant; what remains conscious is the numinosum, the energy that fires our intuition and revitalizes our entire worldview literally from the inside out. In the example of Wilson's awakening, when he conceived of the possibility of a Higher Power as separate from *the Czar of Heaven* and more akin to an energy field, it landed him in the middle of a personal vision quest not unlike Jung's, leading him to discover his vocation and inspiring him to pen the Twelve Steps—his own *myth of expanding consciousness.*[7]

---

[6] Jung, *CW*, Vol. 6, para. 421. The quote reads: "God then becomes an autonomous psychic complex." A psychic complex is an autonomous psychological energy such as the shadow and the Self. The God-image, *the Alcoholic*, and the Trickster are also autonomous psychic complexes, as well as Wilson's "alcoholic mind." We will examine each of these in detail in the coming chapters.

[7] Wilson's journey toward individuation didn't stop with the Big Book and the Twelve Steps. In 1955, he published *Twelve Steps and Twelve Traditions*, an inspired volume wherein he fleshed out the guidelines for group autonomy. Then, in 1962, he presented the Twelve Concepts and the *Service Manual* of A.A., guidelines for those who have been entrusted as servants to the fellowship. Moreover, Wilson considered his own foray into the world of psychedelics as part of his personal adventure, calling

"The Primitive"

In *Psychological Types*, Jung labels the transition of the God-image into an energetic factor a "reversion to *the primitive*," a state of mind similar to what Jaime was seeking when he adopted the myth of the Ajumawi. Such a mindset is a *positive, progressive modification* within the Western psyche that allows one to attain deeper religious insights, to gain a more direct channel to the spiritual energy which underlies every religious symbol since the dawn of consciousness. Importantly, this *ancient attitude* is not derived from the adoption of a religious system of belief from outside of one's own cultural backdrop, "pumping it into one's barren soul," as Jung warned against; instead, *the primitive* grows naturally out of one's genuine confrontation with the God-image, allowing one to unveil the transformative energy hidden within it.

The primitive represents a religious attitude that is not bogged down by the adornments of modern rationale; it is a far more spiritually advanced frame of reference that propels one toward enlightenment. One who arrives at such a state has been catapulted into the highly symbolic realm in which myth is conceived—the objective psyche—from whence one's own *myth of expanding consciousness* may emanate. Recall that Jung had encouraged Jaime to adopt a religious practice that allowed him "to function in a civilized

---

it a "less orthodox path" toward "spiritual progress" in his second letter to Jung, dated March of 1961. Finally, in an interview with Jay Stinnett on November 17, 2023, Lincoln Norton, a teacher of Transcendental Meditation, said that he taught Bill to meditate on December 11, 1969. In the interview, Norton confirms that Bill continued to meditate as much as he was able to until his death in January of 1971.

society without shutting out the primitive,"[8] suggesting that Jaime learn to fuse the antithetical states of mind defined by life in the mountains among the tribe (his spiritual connection to the rocks, the trees, and the rivers) and life in "Western civilization," where everyone's spiritual resolve is really put to the test. For Jung, by 1921, *the primitive* had come to represent an entirely psychologized conception of the God-image, wherein the shape of the symbol has fully retreated back into the unconscious while its affective power, the numinosum, emerges, forming a working relationship with the conscious aspect of the psyche (what he called *ego*). And while Jaime's spirituality certainly appears to have had some of the hallmarks of this vital shift in perspective, without the ability to consistently access *the primitive* in a state of complete abstinence from all mind and mood altering substances, he or any other person will remain unable to maintain his or her connection to its life-changing power.

The religious attitude that Jung, Eckhart, James, and Wilson adopted signified a fluid, relative conception of deity. Like Jaime, it is an attitude that many of us have longed for and attempted to fetch from without when we tried accessing the gods from a religious culture not our own. And yet, for us in the West, it is not until we allow our own image of God to morph into *an energy, a vibration, or a perspective* and less like a *shape, an image, or a set of 12 rules* that the full potential of its transformative power becomes activated in our lives. It is then that a deity once again adopts the attribution of being an all-pervading life-source or power, as it was in

---

[8] Angulo, *Coyotes*, 224.

ancient times and still is in most non-European traditions. The metamorphosis of the God-image is what Jung referred to as its *relativity*, and it has a much deeper history than we might have imagined; for while it has been practiced by Western mystics such as Meister Eckhart, Carl Jung, and Bill Wilson, it originated with our far more ancient spiritual ancestors, such as the Taos and the Ajumawi, predating even the ancient East. Jung explains:

> [The reversion to *the primitive*] was what happened with the mystics [like Eckhart], though it was not the first time that the idea of God's relativity had appeared. It was found in principle and in the very nature of things among [the ancients, who felt] the idea of God has a purely dynamic character; God is a divine force, a power related to health, to the soul, to medicine, to riches, to the chief, a power that can be captured by certain procedures and employed for the making of things needful for the life and well-being of man, and also to produce magical or baneful effects. [The ancient person sensed] this power as much within him as outside him; it was as much his own life force as it is the "medicine" in his amulet, or the mana emanating from his chief...the first demonstrable conception of an all-pervading spiritual force.[9]

---

[9]Jung, *CW*, Vol. 6, paras. 414-415. Jung also wrote, "The return to primeval

Just like what happened with Eckhart and Jung, Wilson allowed his own conception of the God-image to change: Confronted with Ebby's query, "Why don't you choose your own conception of God?" Wilson dropped into *the primitive*, explaining, "I could go for such conceptions as Creative Intelligence, Universal Mind, and Spirit of Nature, but I resisted the thought of the Czar of the Heavens, no matter how loving his sway might be."[10] Wilson's relationship to this newly conceived Cosmic Energy closely resembled a primordial conception of the Divine—a Supreme Power permeating everything in the universe, including himself, which, in his quintessential Western voice, Wilson expressed thusly, "God is either everything, or else he is nothing. God either is or He isn't."[11]

Recognizing that "lack of power"[12] is the great dilemma facing those in most need of divine intervention, Wilson wisely included the notion of *the primitive* in the Step Two: "We came to believe that a power greater than ourselves could restore us to sanity."[13] Wilson astutely pulled from his own experience, knowing that many of his readers, like himself, upon encountering the God-image, would resist a conventional conception of it as he had. Turning our spiritual gaze inward, what emerges is the same *ancient attitude* toward

---

nature and mystic regression to the psychic conditions of prehistory are common to all regions in which the impelling dynamic has not yet petrified into an abstract idea but still is a living experience." Jung, *CW*, vol. 6, para. 431.

[10] *Alcoholics Anonymous*, 12.

[11] *Alcoholics Anonymous*, 52.

[12] *Alcoholics Anonymous*, 45.

[13] *Alcoholics Anonymous*, 59.

the Divine that all humans share in the deepest reaches of the collective unconscious. Wilson demonstrates how we get at such an ancient perspective properly, by allowing it to evolve from out of the mythological rhizome within, thereby addressing our tendency toward agnosticism and accessing the Cosmic Principle that sits just beneath our preconception of the divine. This, in turn, leads us to discover its affective power, to have an encounter with the numinosum.

10

Spiritual Dynamics

When the God-image is relieved of its metaphysical constraints, the numinosum is activated through the tension of psychological opposites that Jung referred to in his 1923 correspondence with Jaime: "In short, you cannot content yourself to live on a paradoxical knife-edge, [the image you adopt] has to symbolize the suitable fusion of the pairs of opposites in a way that makes it possible for you to function in a civilized society without shutting out the primitive."[1] Jung had introduced "the problem of the opposites" in *Psychological Types*—which Jaime read while studying the myth of the Ajumawi. In *Memories, Dreams, Reflections*, Jung recalls reading Goethe's *Faust* as a young man, which "awakened in [him] the problem of opposites, of good and evil, of mind and matter, of light and darkness."[2] During the pivotal years prior to his writing of *Psychological Types*, when Jung was rediscovering his soul, the "problem of opposites" reappeared in the forefront of his mind, becoming a key component in his emerging theory of individuation: "The fact, therefore, that

---

[1] De Angulo, *Coyotes*, 224.
[2] Jung, *MDR*, 235.

a polarity underlies the dynamics of the psyche means that the whole problem of opposites in its broadest sense, with all its concomitant religious and philosophical aspects, is drawn into the psychological discussion."[3] A fusion of the opposites is the aim of every psychological process of transformation, relevant to both individuation as well as Twelve Step recovery.

The Coniunctio Oppositorum

Jung would eventually refer to the strange marriage that occurs through the fusion of the opposing poles in the psyche as *the coniunctio oppositorum*, which means the reconciling, or conjunction, of the opposites. The coniunctio is the restoration of the psyche from the original split that has left us sequestered from our Source. Jung culled many of his ideas regarding the coniunctio from ancient texts of the East as well as Christian mysticism, and developed it alongside his notion of the Self.[4] In *Psychological Types,* Jung introduced a discussion of the coniunctio with help from a quote from one such text, laying the groundwork for what a fusion of the opposites might look like for Westerners:

> The Ramayana says: "This world must suffer under the pairs of opposites forever." Not to allow oneself to be influenced by the pairs of opposites, but to be nirdvandva (free, untouched by the opposites), to raise oneself

---

[3] Jung, *MDR*, 350.
[4] We will examine the Self in more detail beginning in chapter 14.

> above them, is an essentially ethical task, because deliverance from the opposites leads to redemption ... Since suffering is an affect, release from affects means deliverance. Deliverance from the flux of affects, from the tension of opposites, is synonymous with the way of redemption that gradually leads to Brahman. Brahman is thus not only a state but also a process.[5]

As in the East, Jung's psychological model is based upon a play between the opposites: Individuation, like enlightenment, emerges from their conjunction, an *at-one-ment* of the opposing poles in the psyche. Jung understood Brahman to be both the state of having been delivered from the opposites—nirdvandva, free and untouched—as well as the middle way that cuts through them. In like manner, the Twelve Steps also represent a destination as well as the journey of the release from the pair of opposites, *to drink or not to drink*, and an ever-increasing "freedom from the bondage of self"[6] that comes by practicing the Steps as a way of life, "one day at a time." In order to understand the concept of Brahman more clearly, we might imagine that the Steps, the activator of spiritual energy, are *the* Higher Power—the source that leads to the Source—for rising above a charged pair of psychological opposites while passing safely between them is the essence of enlightenment, the aim of *an entire psychic change.*

---

[5] Jung, *CW*, vol. 6, paras. 327, 330.
[6] *Alcoholics Anonymous*, 63.

And while each of us deals with our own unique problem of opposites, the alcoholic—cursed to suffer under a deadly tension defined by the disease *forever*—provides a stark modern example of this universal psychospiritual quandary. Recall that Wilson said that the problem of the alcoholic centers in the mind: Alcoholism thus becomes a telling symbol of the polarity that courses through the human psyche, so fundamental in fact that it is part and parcel of *being*. Psychologists have theorized that the awareness of the polarity that underlies everything in existence is what constitutes consciousness: As one example, Edward Edinger writes, "awareness of the opposites [is] the specific feature of consciousness."[7] The healthy development of the human psyche throughout the course of one's life involves an ever-evolving ability to navigate a world that is permeated with pairs of opposites, the aim of *spirituality* being to cultivate an attitude of neutrality regarding them.

The Cosmos itself is composed of the very same dynamism that courses through our soul and our lives: "Our psyche is set up in accord with the structure of the universe," writes Jung, "and what happens in the macrocosm likewise happens in the infinitesimal and most subjective recesses of the psyche."[8] Viewed in this light, the Cosmos is a looking glass, and staring into the sky on a clear, starry night, we see a mirror of what is taking place behind the veil of consciousness. Science tells us that the energy which permeates the farthest reaches of space as well forms the basis of the subatomic

---

[7] Edinger, *Ego and Archetype*, 18.
[8] Jung, *MDR*, 335.

particles that make up the human nervous system, from there constellating into consciousness. At base, the finding suggests that matter itself is composed of something akin to human consciousness, an idea that Max Plank, the father of quantum physics, had floated as early as 1918: "I regard consciousness as fundamental. I regard matter as derivative from consciousness. We cannot get behind consciousness."[9]

Empirically speaking, then, spiritual power does not emanate from somewhere or something outside of one's own psyche, for the psyche is composed of such energy, derived from the subatomic realm where a person is quite literally one and the same as everything else in the universe. From its place in the psyche, this dynamism funnels into our mythological symbols, seeing that myth is the imprint the collective unconscious has left upon the physical world, "the secret opening through which the inexhaustible energies of the cosmos pour into human cultural manifestation,"[10] as Joseph Campbell wrote in his seminal book, *The Hero With A Thousand Faces*. In our Western myths, this polarity has been expressed through archetypal pairs of opposites: time/ eternity, eternal life/eternal damnation, heaven/hell, good/ evil, God/Satan, natural man/spiritual man, and so on. The God-image, the most poignant Western symbol of Cosmic Energy, is also composed of opposing poles, and the most penetrative, transformative experiences must be built upon a configuration of the opposites that these symbols embody.

---

[9] From an interview with Plank on the 25th of January, 1931.
[10] Joseph Campbell, *The Hero with a Thousand Faces*, 3rd ed, Bollingen Series XVII (Novato, Calif: New World Library, 2008), p. 1.

Since they form the basis of our personal psychology, the opposites define the direction of our unique spiritual path. Jung said that "man cannot conquer the tremendous polarity of his nature on his own resources. He can only do so through the terrifying experience of a psychic process that is independent of himself, that works him rather than he it."[11] That process is the work of an "autonomous psychic complex," the God-image newly conceived as a psychic factor. Encompassing the opposites, the autonomous complex *drives* us from both ends of the psycho-energetic spectrum, through instinctual behavior on one hand and our spiritual vocation on the other—the lowest and the highest of our nature— the essence of the Great Reality. Even though it has been represented throughout the ages by way of myth, due to the autonomous nature of the process, we cannot fully explain it, nor can it be contained or controlled.

The Laws of Spiritual Dynamics

The fundamental polarity inherent deep within the human psyche (and its emergent archetypal imagery) is what gives the transformation process autonomy over the human ego (or the conscious will). Because it is autonomous, the fruits of the numinosum—paradoxical symbols—are not "made" in the traditional sense; they spring forth from the seeds of spiritual potential deep within the Universal Mind, as the energy of the Cosmos blossoms into symbolical shapes of its own accord:[12]

---

[11] Jung, *CW*, vol. 11, para. 446.
[12] Jung explained that "The symbol is alive so long as it is pregnant with meaning... It is, therefore, quite impossible to create a living symbol, i.e.,

I have called this process in its totality the transcendent function, "function" being here understood not as a basic function but as a complex function made up of other functions, and "transcendent" not as denoting a metaphysical quality but merely the fact that this function facilitates a transition from one attitude to another. The raw material shaped by thesis and antithesis, and in the shaping of which the opposites are united, is the living symbol. Its profundity of meaning is inherent in the raw material itself, the very stuff of the psyche, transcending time and dissolution; and its configuration by the opposites ensures its sovereign power over all the psychic functions.[13]

In order to facilitate our understanding of the energizing factor that fuels human transformation, I propose the following two *laws of spiritual dynamics*. The first law states that *archetypal images are the building blocks of consciousness and as such, they form the basis of matter as well.* Recall from last chapter Jung said that "symbols are shaped energies." Here he cleverly calls them "the stuff of the psyche," the "raw material" of consciousness. As the conscious ego evolves, so do its religious images, forming the basis of human perception and the foundation upon which the ego builds

---

one that is pregnant with meaning, from known associations." Jung, *CW*, vol. 6, para. 817.

[13] Jung, *CW*, vol. 6, para. 828.

its defense mechanisms, the protective walls it needs in order to survive the dangerous environment from which it emerged. Thus, these symbols are the foundation of our self-awareness, the lens through which we relate to the universe as conscious individuals in the divine drama of *being*. So, when our conception of the symbols changes, it represents a fundamental shift deep within the psyche, whereby we begin to perceive ourselves and the world around us differently. Furthermore, as the basis of consciousness, the living symbol also forms matter, inasmuch as consciousness is the means through which the universe is granted objective existence.[14] Therefore, when we properly relate to its symbols, Cosmic Energy is unleashed, morphing the material world to suit us as we strive to fulfill our spiritual vocation. Living in accordance with an ever-increasing intensity of spiritual consciousness, we often confront inexplicable, miraculous synchronicities in physis—many of our "wildest dreams come true" as we are led to discover, and then fulfill, our predetermined destiny.

The second law of spiritual dynamics states that *the transformative energy of the psyche is activated by the inherent polarity of the religious archetype, which gives it autonomy over one's attitudes, behaviors, and outward circumstances.* Because these symbols are "configured by the opposites," they have "autonomy over all the psychic functions." The "coincidence of opposites"[15] that manifests in our mythological symbols serves a very important purpose

---

[14] See Jung, *MDR*, p. 252.

[15] C. G. Jung, *Collected Works of C.G. Jung, Volume 8: The Structure and Dynamics of the Psyche,* ed. R. F.C. Hull (Princeton University Press, 2014), para. 679.

for spiritual growth, being the very thing that activates the numinosum. As with an electrical current, where the carefully channeled tension between the negative and positive poles creates energy, when the dynamism between the highest and lowest aspects of our nature is harnessed through a living mythological image, it allows for the flow of spiritual power, propelling us toward transformation. Thus, our most bedeviling problems tend to generate the most spiritual momentum— they require the most energy to counterbalance.

Jung explains that when the energy of the psyche is reconciled in this way, the dilemma is solved, leading to a revolution in every area of life:

> If the mediatory product remains intact, it forms the raw material for a process not of dissolution but of construction, in which [the opposites] both play their part. In this way it becomes a new content that governs the whole attitude, putting an end to the division and forcing the energy of the opposites into a common channel. The standstill is overcome and life can flow on with renewed power towards new goals.[16]

Being composed of the full spectrum of psychic energies, the transcendent process has autonomy over *all* of our psychic functions—*good and bad*—facilitating their at-one-ment by

---

[16] C. G. Jung, *Collected Works of C.G. Jung, Volume 4: Freud & Psychoanalysis*, ed. R. F.C. Hull (Princeton University Press, 2014), paras. 827-28.

harmonizing them in the fulfillment of our spiritual vocation. This powerful process infuses meaning and value into both the highest and the lowest aspects of our being, which becomes a great asset as we try to make ourselves "useful to both God and our fellows."[17] Thus, Wilson encourages us to "cling to the thought that, in God's hands, the dark past is the greatest possession [we] have—the key to life and happiness for others. With it [we] can avert death and misery for them."[18] Embodying the opposites, the numinosum empowers us to reconcile them in whatever form they manifest in our lives, making it fit to overcome any spiritual obstacle we encounter, no matter how deep, dark, or devilish it might be.

Wilson Discovers a Middle Way

Ancient myths in the West have expressed the fundamental polarity, to which all of nature is subject, through the Cosmic symbols of the creation of the world and the birth, death and resurrection of gods and humans. The antithesis is embedded in the archetypal pairs of opposites expressed in symbolical stories, like the Garden of Eden and the Crucifixion of Christ. The myth of the Twelve Steps expresses the dichotomy the same way it does every mythological truth—stripped of the cumbersome dogmatic language that has tainted the older stories, placing the Anonymous Alcoholic center stage, cast in the lead role in a modern drama of opposites. Now, a deadly psychological conflict is presented as the plot of the story,

---

[17] *Alcoholics Anonymous*, 76.
[18] *Alcoholics Anonymous*, 124.

expressed by the juxtaposition of the behavior over which one is powerless, such as drinking or using drugs, with the solution, i.e., sobriety, which our hero can only attain through having "a vital spiritual experience." The demons one faces along the way are of one's own making, while the goal of the journey moves one toward a completely new perspective of one's place in the world. Like all religious symbols, recovery from alcoholism or addiction by spiritual means manifests as an unlikely fusion of a pair of opposites, impossible to describe, pregnant with meaning, and imbued with so much paradoxicality that it can only be fully appreciated by those having lived through it.

In the Steps, the cosmic symbols of eternal salvation and damnation have been reduced to the perplexing behavior that the Anonymous Alcoholic is compelled to engage in, which eventually becomes so bad that "only a spiritual experience can conquer [it]."[19] Wilson wrote about this terrible dilemma for the alcoholic, who faces certain devastation if he goes on drinking: "To continue on as he is means disaster, especially if he is an alcoholic of the hopeless variety. To be doomed to an alcoholic death or to live on a spiritual basis are not always easy alternatives to face."[20] As ridiculous as that sentence might sound to the unaffected, Wilson was being dead serious when he wrote it. The opposites are so polarized within the psyche that in the alcoholic mythos, the result of failing to reconcile them is not only a state of spiritual death (as symbolized in the ancient myths), but often includes the literal death

---

[19] *Alcoholics Anonymous*, 44.
[20] *Alcoholics Anonymous*, 44.

of the individual, so common nowadays, caused from the stranglehold of addiction. Wilson writes, "With us, to drink is to die,"[21] and anyone familiar with the Twelve Step fellowships knows that Wilson was not being dramatic in saying it: The spiritual death of the alcoholic/addict very often manifests in the most tragic ways in real life as well. "Buy a black suit or dress" is one of the first suggestions given to newcomers in a Twelve Step fellowship; those of us who survived the ordeal have countless friends who weren't so lucky.

And while Wilson didn't shy away from describing the harsh consequences of relapse in outer life, he understood well that the solution to "the tremendous polarity" of one's nature is found inside—through an autonomous process that takes place in the depths of the soul. And yet, rather than damning the negative component of alcoholism and addiction as an "unintegratable evil,"[22] as one author has done, Wilson takes an entirely different tact, one which nonalcoholics might easily overlook—one that echoes Jung's suggestion to Jaime that he learn to fuse the opposites of "the paradoxical knife-edge" that had come to define his life. For while it is imperative that alcoholics "stay away from drink," like every impossible dilemma that humans are forced to endure, the way in which they do so is a complete paradox, making it difficult to understand or describe, even for those who have experienced it. *How does one conjoin the opposing states of drunkenness and sobriety when so much emphasis needs to*

---

[21] *Alcoholics Anonymous*, 44, 66.

[22] David E. Schoen, *The War of the Gods in Addiction: C.G. Jung, Alcoholics Anonymous, and Archetypal Evil* (Asheville, North Carolina: Chiron Publications, 2020).

be placed on the "not drinking" part? Many alcoholics admit that they were only able to finally quit drinking after they had given up, deciding that they were unable to do so and were fated to join the unlucky sots who "died drunk," further highlighting the paradoxical nature of the insoluble conflict of which we speak.

Wilson understood that "bottles were only a symbol,"[23] that for alcoholics, the antinomy between the states of drunkenness and sobriety is in reality a reflection of the interior human condition, where a cosmogonic war is being waged. Jung said that "the heart of man is filled with raging battle,"[24] and while it is true that "every person must suffer under the pairs of opposites forever," as the ancient text says, such a struggle seems to be far more evident in the lives of those desperate enough to work a Twelve Step program. For all of us, the battleground lies right where our opposing tendencies meet, which within the context of the Twelve Steps happens in Step One. Yet, notice how Wilson describes his new perspective toward the liquid that nearly caused his ultimate demise once he had experienced the paradoxical process of awakening: He demonstrates an attitude akin to that of Brahman—having been delivered from the tension of

---

[23] Jung takes this thought even further when he says that projected symbols are symptomatic of living in an unconscious state: "If there is a subordination of one part, the symbol will be predominantly the product of the other part, and, to that extent, less a symbol than a symptom—a symptom of the suppressed antithesis." Jung, *CW*, vol. 6, para. 824. An outwardly projected symbol of God, which one spends their life seeking but never attaining, is reflective of an inner state of longing.

[24] Jung, *CW*, vol. 6, para. 114. The quote in its entirety: "The heart of man is 'filled with raging battle,' says Julian the Apostate."

opposites—coupled with a Zenlike approach to life in general, being fully present, living "one day at a time," a truly surprising resting point for a broke, broken and newly sober New York City stockbroker:

> And we have ceased fighting anything or anyone—even alcohol. At this point, sanity will have returned. We will seldom be interested in liquor. If tempted, we recoil from it as from a hot flame. We react sanely and normally, and we will find that this has happened automatically. We will see that our new attitude toward liquor has been given us without any thought or effort on our part. It just comes! That is the miracle of it. We are not fighting it, neither are we avoiding temptation. *We feel as though we had been placed in a position of neutrality— safe and protected. We have not even sworn off. Instead, the problem has been removed. It does not exist for us. We are neither cocky nor are we afraid. That is our experience.* That is how we react so long as we keep in fit spiritual condition.[25]

Wilson's description of recovery from alcoholism has earmarks of Jungian individuation and the tenor of "nirdvandva (free, untouched by the opposites)." Jung explained that for this kind of psychological process to unfold, the opposites "have to be

---

[25] *Alcoholics Anonymous*, 84-85. Italics mine.

clearly separated so that their positive and negative aspects become visible. Only thus can we take up a middle position and discover a middle way."[26] Sadly, for many alcoholics and addicts, the opposites do not become visible until it is too late, and the situation becomes so dire that it threatens one's sanity and one's life. Whether one is alcoholic or not, for a middle way to appear, it takes a crisis of such magnitude that the ego, against its very nature, finally gives up hope of ever trying to solve it. Thus, the journey of a sober alcoholic becomes the prototype of the passage through any pair of psychological opposites that men and women face today: Step One delineates the negative aspect of the dilemma, where powerlessness is the lash that drives one to the breaking point, where one finally realizes that a transcendent power is needed to solve the problem. And yet, instead of instructing a person how to quit drinking, which is what *we had all* expected Wilson to do, the remaining 11 steps reveal a psychospiritual process one might adopt in order to create "a new attitude," i.e., to achieve deliverance from the insoluble conflict represented by the ism of alcohol. Such a highly evolved spiritual consciousness is the state of heaven on earth we've all wished for—what in the East is called *enlightenment.*

---

[26] Cited in Edward F. Edinger, *The New God-Image: A Study of Jung's Key Letters Concerning the Evolution of the Western God-Image*, eds. Dianne D. Cordic and Charles Yates (Asheville, North Carolina: Chiron Publications, 2015), pp. 113-114.

Part Three

The Thirst for Wholeness

11

The Archetype of *The Alcoholic*

Despite tremendous growth in the first three decades of their existence, neither AA nor the Big Book seems to have ever really caught Carl Jung's attention, so far as we know, until Wilson's brief correspondence with him in January of 1961.[1] Although the Twelve Steps remained relatively unknown, by that time AA had grown exponentially, having bloomed to over 300,000 members and more than 8,000 groups worldwide, with many other Twelve Step fellowships forming and expanding quickly.[2] For example, NA, Al-Anon and Alateen (a group for teenage children of alcoholics) had already been around for nearly a decade, and GA (Gamblers Anonymous) half that, with dozens of other iterations soon to follow, each with Wilson's heartfelt support and appreciation.

---

[1] Amy Colwell Bluhm offers evidence that Jung had heard about AA in the 1940s, through a mutual acquaintance, Margarita Littichau. There is even some correspondence between the Wilson and Littichau. See Bluhm, Amy Colwell, "Verification of C.G. Jung's analysis of Rowland hazard and the history of Alcoholics Anonymous," American Psychological Association 2006, Vol. 9, No. 4.

[2] As of 2024, AA alone is estimated to have over 2,000,000 members and over 180,000 groups in 100 plus countries worldwide.

The correspondence between Wilson and Jung has added greatly to our understanding of the psychospiritual quandary in which the alcoholic is trapped as a byproduct of the spiritual crisis we face in the West. In the letter Wilson wrote to Jung, he offered gratitude for Jung's contribution to AA and the Twelve Steps, expressing his admiration of the doctor for the advice he had given his patient Rowland Hazard to seek "a vital spiritual experience." Wilson told Jung that along with the contents of James's *The Varieties of Religious Experience* and the "verdict of hopelessness" Dr. Silkworth had pronounced upon him (Wilson), Jung's message had become one of the pillars upon which Alcoholics Anonymous was built. Jung's health was already ailing by that time; thankfully, he had strength enough to respond to Wilson's first letter.[3] Lamentably, Jung would die only a few months later.

We've seen how Jung had intuited fairly early in his career that alcoholism is at base an issue of spiritual connection (or lack thereof), and his letter to Bill paints an even clearer picture than what we have in those brief, early communications. There Jung presents Rowland's immense craving for liquor as a tangible symbol of an intangible, spiritual thirst:

> [Rowland's] craving for alcohol was the
> equivalent, on a low level, of the spiritual

---

[3] Two of the letters can be found in the Grapevine article from 1963: *The Bill W. - Carl Jung Letters*, January 1963, Alcoholics Anonymous, "The AA Grapevine." Hereafter, *Grapevine*. Jung's letter to Wilson can also be found in Jung, *Letters*, vol. 2, p. 623-24. Part of Wilson's second letter to Jung can be found in *Pass It On.*

> thirst of our being for wholeness, expressed
> in medieval language: the union with God.
> How could one formulate such an insight in
> a language that is not misunderstood in our
> days?[4]

While both Jung and Wilson tie alcoholism to an underlying spiritual condition that requires a transcendent religious experience to conquer, here Jung clarifies that the spiritual malady that sits at the core of alcoholism is not peculiar to alcoholics; it is, in fact, universal. As a postscript to the letter, Jung cites a scripture as the basis for his metaphor of the intangible spiritual thirst, the beautiful Psalm 42:1: "As the heart panteth after the water brooks, so panteth my soul after thee, O God." Thus, Jung conveys that just as humans instinctually thirst for clean, fresh water, we too have a similar (often unconscious) thirst for connection with the Divine. And for those who are alcoholic, that longing manifests outwardly as an insatiable craving for "the effect produced by alcohol"[5]—something we imagine Jung might have witnessed firsthand with Jaime as they traversed the desolate canyonlands between Grand Canyon and Taos.

An Archetype Emerges

The universality of our "spiritual thirst for wholeness" permits us to view Wilson's central character in the Big Book as a

---

[4] Jung, *Letters*, vol. 2, p. 624.
[5] *Alcoholics Anonymous*, xxviii.

metaphor of our unfulfilled longing for union with God. In this light, the Anonymous Alcoholic reflects our failed hope to reach the Divine, just as the characters of the ancient myths are meant to do. And as with all religious symbols, there is an ancient energy underlying the Anonymous Alcoholic that, in the Jungian tradition, I have named the archetype of *the Alcoholic*, a paradoxical figure representative of the fusion of opposites that takes place in recovery.

Broadly speaking, the mysticism surrounding intoxication is evidence of the presence of *the Alcoholic*—anytime we seek a transformative spiritual experience induced through intoxication, whether that be through using psychedelics or some other intoxicant, we are channeling the power of the archetype.[6] For example, the practice now in vogue in some post-Jungian circles of using mind- or mood-altering substances to enhance the analytical process evidences the presence of the archetype of *the Alcoholic*. Another example is found in Michael Pollan's bestselling book *How to Change Your Mind*, where he makes a strong case for the use of psychedelics as a means to enhance one's spiritual consciousness—further evidence of the energy of *the Alcoholic* at work in the modern psyche. Even William James seems to have been swayed by the archetype of *the Alcoholic*; using

---

[6] From the Greek God Dionysus, to the Miller in the Canterbury Tales, to Shakespeare's John Falstaff, to Walter White in the famous modern television series "Breaking Bad," *the Alcoholic* archetype appears in many of our culture's most beloved fictional characters, ancient and modern, where it depicts the enhanced powers of the mind and spirit believed to accompany those who have a penchant for hard drink and/or the company of criminals.

nitrous oxide as a way to access the mystical, he quotes the Russian novelist Leo Tolstoy in *Varieties*, "One can live only so long as one is intoxicated, drunk with life; but when one grows sober one cannot fail to see that it is all a stupid cheat."[7] Finally, we mustn't overlook either Wilson's foray into the world of psychedelics in the 1950s, or Jaime's in the early 1920s, as other clear cases of the power of this paradoxical image and the inevitable shortcomings of reliance on this method alone to quench the intangible "thirst of our being for wholeness." For, while imbibing any kind of intoxicant certainly evokes an expansion of consciousness, the fullness of the archetype of *the Alcoholic* cannot be experienced unless we find a way to improve our conscious contact with the Universal Mind while in a state of abstinence, as James intimated.

In its negative aspect, *the Alcoholic* archetype is what inspires our misguided attempts to fulfill what Jung told Wilson is "an unrecognized spiritual need." But *the Alcoholic* is also reflective of the safe passage through the middle of the crisis of opposites that defines every spiritual dilemma—the hero's journey inward as well as the sense of completeness which comes to one who has successfully fused the opposing states of whatever insoluble conflict had them trapped. As an image of wholeness, the archetype of *the Alcoholic* entails coming full circle, reconnecting to a Higher Power, and progressively unifying one's inner and outer worlds. In Twelve Step meetings, when we introduce ourselves with the phrase, "My name is Bill, and I'm an alcoholic" or "I'm Debbie, I'm an addict," without knowing it, we are summoning the

---

[7] James, *Varieties*, 118.

power of this archetype—a "grateful alcoholic" is one who has unknowingly tapped into the transformative energies of the archetype of *the Alcoholic* and thereby "recovered from a seemingly hopeless state of mind and body."[8]

Wilson's intuition in making the central figure in the Big Book an anonymous alcoholic meant that it could be reinterpreted in a broad fashion, having already found expression in over 400 sister fellowships and counting, each with its own unique iteration of the Twelve Steps dealing with a specific addiction or behavioral issue other than alcoholism. The archetypal nature of the Anonymous Alcoholic allows for an accompanying fellowship for the nonaddicted friends and family of those affected as well, such as Al-Anon, Nar-Anon, and Gam-Anon. Moreover, some fellowships, such as CA (Cocaine Anonymous) and HA (Heroin Anonymous), use the book *Alcoholics Anonymous* as their "basic text," forgoing the need to alter the message as it flowed from Wilson's pen. So, when members in those fellowships tell their stories about their struggle with powerlessness over substances or behaviors other than alcohol, they understand the words *alcohol*, *alcoholic*, and *alcoholism* to reflect aspects of their own unique spiritual dilemma. The archetypal nature of *the Alcoholic* accounts for why sects from every major religion have adopted the Twelve Steps as a spiritual practice for their members who struggle with certain compulsive behaviors or addictions, some even modifying the Twelve Steps to align with their own religious dogma. However, since they lack the psychological approach toward the God-image that

---

[8] *Alcoholics Anonymous*, 20.

Wilson carefully formulated (concurrently with Jung), and since they do not adhere to the Twelve Traditions—Wilson's official statement on the nature and importance of individual anonymity and group autonomy—it is questionable how successful those iterations are in treating "the real alcoholic."

Alcoholism and the West's Spiritual Crisis

It has been our culture's lack of an effective, living connection to myth that gave rise to the prevailing sociospiritual condition that constellates the negative aspect of archetype of *the Alcoholic* throughout the world. The scale at which the disease of alcoholism has inflicted the West is indicative of just how hollow our relationship to our God-image has become, how waning the health of our religions, whose message has lost its meaning and value. The American Indians of the Great Plains provide a disturbing case in point of how the lack of connection to a meaningful mythology can lead to a sweeping outbreak of alcoholism and addiction like the one we are witnessing today: After the U.S. government decimated the Native's God-image—systematically slaughtering the sacred Buffalo—alcoholism emerged among the tribes as a widespread chronic illness. Having witnessed the murder of their mythological symbols, the tribespeople lost a vital connection with the Great Spirit, and in their longing to find what went missing, a deadly and destructive compulsion emerged from the depths of their collective unconscious, erupting into a culturewide epidemic.

Likewise, in the West, the widespread nature of the disease of alcoholism is highly reflective of the anemic state

155

of our current, collective spiritual well-being, stemming from our inability to reconcile our myths with a modern, scientific worldview. Jung discovered this phenomenon poking through the writings of Friedrich Nietzsche, who had boldly declared that the West no longer needed access to a living God-image. In a lecture series he presented in the spring of 1934 on Nietzsche's philosophical novel, *Thus Spoke Zarathustra*, Jung explored the psychology around Nietzsche's denial of the thirst for wholeness, which diverted the energy of the numinosum, causing it to bubble up from the unconscious through its negative aspect—in the form of an acute neurosis—which, Jung says, Nietzsche then unconsciously projected into the characters of his fiction. Observing the impact of this spiritual malaise among those who showed a tendency toward substance abuse, Jung explained:

> Spirit is also the source of inspiration and of enthusiasm, because it is a welling-up; the German word Geist [i.e., Spirit] is a volcanic eruption, a geyser. That aspect of the spirit is the reason why alcohol, for instance, is called spirit: alcohol is the reduced form of spirit. Therefore many people, lacking spirit, take to drink. They fill themselves with alcohol; I have seen many a case of that sort. It is typical for men, though women do it too.[9]

---

[9] C. G. Jung and James L. Jarrett, *Jung's Seminar on Nietzsche's Zarathustra*, abridged ed., Bollingen Series 99 (Princeton, N.J: Princeton University Press, 1998) vol. 2: 1039. Hereafter *Zarathustra*.

As a culture's religious myths lose sway, a compensating energy wells up in the collective psychology, as overpowering primordial forces meant to drive us toward wholeness emanate from a darker, more archaic aspect in the psyche, influencing certain individuals so profoundly that they become acutely neurotic, which often manifests as alcoholism and/or addiction. Thus, in addition to the spiritual implications we've been examining that are necessary for one to achieve a full recovery from the disease, a corresponding spiritual basis colors the dark and compulsive behavior that defines active alcoholism as well. Understanding that, Jung explained that the best treatment for such neurotic, addictive states is found in "cultivating a symbolic life," encouraging us to find a way to address what he calls "the daily need of the soul."[10]

The Alcoholic and the Trickster

Bill Wilson's statement that "bottles are a symbol" underscores the universal nature of our spiritual thirst for wholeness. From a psychological perspective, the drama that his character endures is the same journey symbolized by every Western myth: The mechanism in the mind that deludes the Anonymous Alcoholic into thinking he "will somehow, someday, control and enjoy his drinking"[11] is the same one that tricks all of us into believing that our ego is steering the ship, that we have ultimate control over every aspect of our lives. An unconscious compulsion to drink is what finally

---

[10] Jung, *CW*, vol. 18, para. 627. This is the same talk where Jung made a reference to Rowland Hazard and the Oxford Group.
[11] *Alcoholics Anonymous*, 30.

leads alcoholics to experience what Wilson called (in his letter to Jung) "ego collapse at depth." All humans are driven by unconscious compulsions. Indeed, to be human means to encounter compulsivity—Jung says that compulsion is the most baffling aspect of our existence, "the great mystery of human life."[12] For while the ego might think it is always in charge, in fact, there is another psychic complex that does most of the driving, which Jung called *the shadow*, and similar to how it manifested in Nietzsche's *Zarathustra*, that shadow complex, typically hidden, is often quite visible in the life of a chronic alcoholic. Therefore, one of the primary functions of the archetype of *the Alcoholic* is to illuminate the shadowy, compulsive parts of our psyche that are eclipsed by a delusion of control.

In the Big Book, Wilson describes the alcoholic dilemma as a "self-imposed crisis *that we could not postpone or evade*."[13] As the dilemma deepens, alcoholics are forced to delude themselves more and more to justify behaving in ways that contradict their values, chipping away at their moral character. Sometimes they set their moral compass aside when they are under the influence, but real "self-imposed" psychological damage is done when they do so in a state of abstinence, in order to get more booze. At first, they fool themselves into thinking that they choose to behave in such a self-destructive way. But the truth is far more insidious, for they are really being compelled by a shadow complex tied to an archetype Jung aptly named "the Trickster," in a 1954 essay

---

[12] Jung, *CW*, vol. 14, para. 151.
[13] *Alcoholics Anonymous*, 53. Italics mine.

titled "On the Psychology of the Trickster Figure." The Trickster, an ancient variation of the archetype of *the Alcoholic*, bedevils us into believing we are making choices when really we are being driven by the element of unconscious instinct—the intangible thirst for union with God. And since this particular facet of the shadow complex is so apparent in the life of an alcoholic, there is a clear correlation between the typical "alcoholic" trope and the "shadow figure" of the Trickster: both represent "a summation of all the inferior traits of character in individuals."[14]

Comparing Jung's commentary on the Trickster to the archetype of *the Alcoholic* thus helps to illuminate the compulsive parts of the psyche that tend to remain hidden from the ego's view. Jung said of the Trickster that it is "half animal, half divine,"[15] something that can also be said of *the Alcoholic* archetype, considering just how savage its animalistic half can be. *The Alcoholic* sets a deadly trap in alcoholics' lives meant to awaken them to an awareness of their intangible spiritual thirst—if it doesn't kill them first. We see this same disregard for the ego's suffering (as well as for life itself) in the machinations of the Trickster who, playing a similar role in the spiritual awakening, masterminds the debacle that reveals our unconscious longing for wholeness: "Only out of disaster can the longing for the savior arise," writes Jung, "in other words, the recognition and unavoidable integration of the shadow create such a harrowing situation that nobody but

---

[14] Jung, *CW*, vol. 9i, para. 484.
[15] Jung, *CW*, vol. 9i, para. 456.

a savior can undo the tangled web of fate."[16] In the mythos of *the Alcoholic*, the bottle becomes a symbol of the deadly weapon that the trickster complex assaults us with, as it tries to "beat us into a state of reasonableness"[17] regarding our need to relinquish the delusion of control. Uninterested in whether one survives the attack, *the Alcoholic* archetype is only concerned with collapsing the ego; regardless if they live or die, alcoholics are fated to encounter the awful image of themselves in the mirror held up by the objective psyche. As harrowing as it sounds, according to those who made it safely through, it was worth the risk, for it brings with it a tremendous gift—the ability to comprehend the Great Reality and to enjoy the world from the perspective of one who has died spiritually and been "reborn."[18]

Spiritus Contra Spiritum

The mythos of *the Alcoholic* illustrates how the human need for genuine spiritual connection only becomes apparent after one escapes the deadly psychological trap set by the Trickster, under the villainous guise of "managing well."[19] The web that Fate uses to ensnare alcoholics is woven of the same paradoxical thread that comprises everything in the universe, and as the alcoholic drama unfolds, they discover that the only panacea is found in *a fusion of the opposites*—exactly what Jung referred to when he encouraged Jaime to integrate

---

[16] Jung, *CW*, vol. 9i, para. 487.
[17] *Alcoholics Anonymous*, 47-48.
[18] *Alcoholics Anonymous*, 63.
[19] *Alcoholics* Anonymous, 62.

his conception of *the primitive* in his quest to carve out a meaningful role for himself in Western culture. Jung explains further in the Wilson letter:

> You see, Alcohol in Latin is "spiritus," and you use the same word for the highest religious experience as well as for the most depraving poison. The helpful formula therefore is: *spiritus contra spiritum*.[20]

Spiritus contra spiritum is typically understood to mean "to counter alcoholism with spirituality." And yet, the phrase suggests far more than what a perfunctory translation of the Latin would imply: It is an adage regarding the paradoxical nature of the coniunctio that takes place in recovery from alcoholism. Expressive of the union of opposites embodied by the archetype of *the Alcoholic, spiritus contra spiritum* refers to the conjunction of the highest religious experience with that of the most depraved human condition. This means that the negative aspect of the archetype of *the Alcoholic*, which spurs one on to commit what will be atrocious acts, becomes the cornerstone upon which their spiritual experience is built, the pathology itself integral to their quest for enlightenment. Jung explains, "Inasmuch as you attain to the numinous experiences you are released from the curse of pathology. Even the very disease takes on a numinous character."[21] As they begin to

---

[20] Jung, *Letters*, vol. 2, p. 625.

[21] Jung, *Letters*, vol. 1, p. 377. One "attains to the numinous" by adopting a relative perspective of the God-image as well as one's psychic complexes. A psychic complex is any number of "autonomous" functions in the psyche, including alcoholism and addiction as well as one's spiritual vocation.

attribute both the conflict as well as the solution to the driving force of the numinosum—part and parcel of their personal adventure—alcoholics awaken to the notion that what they had hoped to assuage through spirits can only be fully sated by union with *Spiritus,* at which point their entire life becomes imbued with meaning and value, including their dark history in active alcoholism.

The poles that *the Alcoholic* archetype encompasses, of the highest religious experience and the lowest, most depraved human condition, can be categorized as instinct and Spirit, "the most polar [psychological] opposites imaginable," writes Jung.[22] These two extremes constellate within the Trickster as well, which has a 70,000-plus-year history. As such, the Trickster is humankind's oldest archetypal image, reflecting "an extremely *primitive* state of consciousness solidified into a mythological personage."[23] Since the archetype of *the Alcoholic* belongs to the same fundamental pair of psychological opposites, it too personifies "the conflict between the two dimensions of consciousness [and] of the

---

[22] Jung, *CW*, vol. 9i, para. 406.

[23] Jung, *CW*, vol. 9i, para. 474. On account of its relationship to the primordial Trickster image, the archetype of *the Alcoholic* may be responsible not just for the evolution of many different types of spiritual practices throughout the ages of human existence, but for the emergence of consciousness itself. It is worthy of note that the so-called *Stoned Ape Theory*, "first presented by Robert Fischer and then popularized by Terence McKenna [states that] ingestion of psilocybin caused a rapid development of the hominid brain for analytical thinking and societal bonding." Michael Pollan further states that no fewer than 23 "primates (including humans) consume mushrooms and know how to distinguish 'good' from 'bad.'" Pollan, *How to Change your Mind*, pp. 97-98.

polaristic structure of the psyche, which like any other energic system is dependent on the tension of opposites."[24]

Humankind's highest religious aspirations grow directly out of that "tension of opposites." As people who live on a "paradoxical knife edge," primal instinct becomes the driving force behind alcoholics' spiritual quest. Driven to use alcohol as if by an instinctual thirst for union with God, they would do (almost) anything, no matter how stupid, immoral, or degrading, to recapture the "sense of ease and comfort which comes at once by taking a few drinks."[25] And yet, paradoxically, it is their willingness to sacrifice everything worthwhile upon the altar of intoxication that conditions them to a similar compulsive drive toward *Spiritus.* Alcoholics are "Jekyll and Hyde" characters who do "absurd, incredible, tragic things"[26] as long as they remain unconsciously identified with *the Alcoholic* archetype. But once they finally relinquish their delusion of control over alcohol, admitting that they are powerless, they open themselves up to turning their *entire will and life* over to the care of Spiritus, as suggested in Step Three.

The Wounded Healer

According to the second law of spiritual dynamics, the archetype of *the Alcoholic* has *autonomy over all of the psychic functions,* which is why alcoholics tend to "do everything alcoholically" and why when they have a spiritual awakening,

---

[24] Jung, *CW,* vol. 9i, para. 474, 483. Italics mine.
[25] *Alcoholics Anonymous* xxviii.
[26] *Alcoholics Anonymous,* 21.

it usually revolutionizes their entire life, inside and out. Having been led directly into the depths of the psyche by the evil spirits contained in the bottle (*spiritum*), the alcoholic emerges with a spiritual vocation to guide others toward *Spiritus (the breath of life or the Holy Spirit)*. A similar dynamic plays out in indigenous cultures, ancient and modern, where the trickster of the tribe is often called to be its medicine man or woman, having learned to integrate the more depraved parts of themselves. Jung says, "There is something of the trickster in the character of the shaman and medicine-man, [he is] the wounded wounder [who becomes] the agent of healing, the sufferer [who] takes away suffering … [and] who turns the meaningless into the meaningful."[27] By overcoming one's own demons, the shaman learns from practical experience how to guide others to do the same. Escaping a previous way of life dominated by instinct, the shaman masters the magic art of healing, which in the context of spirituality is only discovered by ingesting the *most degrading poison* (metaphorically speaking). *The Alcoholic* is thus a shape-shifter, and as the carrier of spiritual boons, becomes "the symbol of the savior, the bringer of healing"[28] to the tribe—an element of which clearly constellated in Wilson's mind when he devised the Anonymous Alcoholic's heroic adventure through the Twelve Steps, ending with his 12th suggestion that after one has had a spiritual awakening, one carries a message of wholeness to others suffering a similar fate.

---

[27] Jung, *CW*, vol. 9i, para. 457-8.
[28] Jung, *CW*, vol. 9ii, para. 38. See Donald Kalsched, *The Inner World of Trauma: Archetypal Defenses of the Personal Spirit*. (Repr. London: Routledge, 1998)

As an image of wholeness, *the Alcoholic* archetype encompasses the utter darkness and depravity of the most loathsome human condition, but it also represents a metamorphosis, assuming humanity's highest spiritual aspirations *at the same time*. The antithetical nature of archetypal images such as *the Alcoholic* and the Trickster elucidate how deeply dependent we are upon the tension of opposites within the psyche for "an entire psychic change" to occur. Painful though it is, the terrible dilemma unleashed by *the Alcoholic* is what ultimately leads to wholeness, no matter how lost or unconscious one might have been. Like the Trickster, *the Alcoholic* is "a negative hero who manages to achieve through stupidity what others fail to accomplish with their best efforts."[29] Once overrun by the instinctual, amoral aspect of their own humanity, sober alcoholics have undeservedly— as if by divine accident—redeemed themselves, stumbling upon a path to authentic spirituality in the midst of a culture where the ancient wisdom of searching for meaning and value within the darkest parts of one's own being has all but vanished. By bringing with them an irrational cure, they inadvertently shapeshift into real-life shamans, having gained the knowledge of how to help those whom modern medicine, psychiatry, and religion are unable to reach. Being fooled first by the trickster in their own minds, and later their sponsors (who also embody the shamanistic element of the Trickster), sober alcoholics reconcile what was previously irreconcilable within them, fumbling their way toward enlightenment, with the calling to help others do the same.

---

[29] Jung, *CW*, vol. 9i, para. 456.

THE SHADOW OF A FIGURE OF LIGHT

The Music of Alcoholics Anonymous

Throughout the millennia, the Trickster has been variously portrayed as a joker, a court jester, and even a clown, urging us from the depths to find the humor in life's pathos. Now, in the modern costume that the Trickster has donned, that of *the Alcoholic*, he brings a similar levity to the role, discovered in "the music of Alcoholics Anonymous," as the sounds of laughter and joyousness that reverberate through the fellowship hall. Visitors to the space, seeing this display, sometimes wonder whether they haven't just continued "the party" in a state of abstinence; and yet, the chthonic nature of their revelry, while it may be uncomfortable at first, has a profound healing effect, for it dismantles the negative charge of the conflict that plagues them, who have suffered too long in darkness and isolation.

Wilson sensed the healing that takes place in the festive atmosphere of a fellowship of sober drunks long before Alcoholics Anonymous was officially formed, recognizing the obvious paradox embedded within his newfound joy in liberation from spirits: "So we think cheerfulness and laughter make for usefulness. Outsiders are sometimes shocked when we burst into merriment over a seemingly tragic experience out of the past. But why shouldn't we laugh? We have recovered, and have been given the power to help others."[30] That same laughter is heard "in the rooms" today, as modern shamans recite the tragi-comedic tale as old as humankind: *what we used to be like, what happened, and what we are like now.*

---

[30] *Alcoholics Anonymous*, 132.

Jung said that the antidotes of the Trickster, the stories of his journey into the darkness, leave us "to wonder what happened to his evil qualities."[31] Likewise, the modern alcoholics' metamorphoses are aided through the keen sense of humor they adopt regarding some of the most tragic moments of their past, which they then use with surgical precision in order to cut open the heart and mind of a newcomer just enough for the gift of self-acceptance to begin to seep in. So it is that they harness the ancient archetypal energy, as laughter and tears sometimes collide in a single sentence.

And while it's perfectly normal, when faced with such a paradox, to assume that the side that represents *the highest religious experience* has more spiritual meaning and value than what we gain through experiencing *the most depraved poison*, both provide necessary and enduring lessons that become useful tools as we try to help others in the fulfillment of our newfound spiritual trade, "to carry the message." *The Alcoholic* archetype, an image of wholeness, teaches us that neither is more important than the other: Jung wisely states that, ethically speaking, "both can be both."[32] The experience we garner while letting our instinct for ease and comfort lead us to the very gates of hell will have just as much impact upon our continued spiritual and psychological growth as anything we learn when we finally discover heaven on earth. The archetype of *the Alcoholic* reveals that the way to reconcile the opposites is to learn to see them as intrinsic to our nature, regardless of how they manifest in the outside world, and to

---

[31] Jung, *CW*, vol. 9i, para. 477.
[32] Jung, *CW*, vol. 9i, para. 406.

look for the gift of transformation hidden within the worst parts of ourselves. Urging us to set things right whenever we have caused harm, *the Alcoholic* then beckons us to view our own darkness akin to the way we regard the negative charge of electricity, vital to the creation of the spiritual power needed to carry us forward.

12

The Devil

By offering a glimpse into the hidden dynamics of the psyche, archetypal religious images reveal the nature of the fundamental opposition embedded within. So far, we've encountered those energies in the Trickster and *the Alcoholic*. But there is another primary opposition that Jung mentioned in his letter to Bill which also figures heavily into the psychology of the modern West, reflected in the cosmic conflict between Almighty God, *the Czar of Heaven*, and God's archnemesis, the Devil, the purveyor of evil. Like the other symbolical forms we've already covered, these characters of Western myth are images that the Universal Mind produces to express the transformative energy of the Cosmos in a way that our egos might be able to more fully comprehend.[1] Psychologically speaking, our myths, resplendent with tales of "good" against "evil"—and characters who personify such—are projections of energies emanating from "deep down in every man, woman, and child." Jung taught that the evil we see in the world is rooted within us as well; thus, the Devil is as much a part

---

[1] In chapter 14, we will discuss what exactly is meant by the term "ego" and its relationship to the other psychic complexes Jung described.

of our individual makeup as the God-image, and there is no escaping this uncomfortable fact.[2]

In one of his most important works, *Answer to Job* (published in 1952), Jung tells us that the Devil is yet another variation of the primordial Trickster, and as the only being in the universe to "have Yahweh's ear," he is "a spoilsport who loves nothing more than to cause annoying accidents" for Yahweh's children (as he did with the embattled Job).[3] And while *Answer to Job* represents one of Jung's deepest dives into the psychology behind the traditional deities of conventional Western myth, it wasn't his only foray into the underlying question of good versus evil. In many ways, Jung spent his whole career unraveling the significance of the psychological energy represented by such imagery.

The Power of Evil in Twelve Step Mythology

We've already seen that when Jung wrote *Psychological Types* in 1921, he had begun to explore the problem of opposites, including the dark energies of the unconscious. In his letter to Wilson, Jung introduced the Devil into his discussion about alcoholism, paving the way for us to weave a psychological

---

[2] Jung said that "the side we call the Devil ... dwells in the heart," further explaining that "With a little self-criticism one can see through the shadow—so far as its nature is personal. But when it appears as an archetype, one encounters the same difficulties as with anima and animus. In other words, it is quite within the bounds of possibility for a man to recognize the relative evil of his nature, but it is a rare and shattering experience for him to gaze into the face of absolute evil." Jung, *CW*, vol. 5, para. 89 and Jung, *CW*, vol. 9ii, para. 19.
[3] Jung, *CW*, vol. 11, paras. 594, 619.

conception of that dark image into our own spiritual journey. But Jung recognized how challenging such a task can be, admitting to Wilson that the Devil is a widely misconstrued symbol even when it's not being used in conjunction with a miscomprehended mental illness like alcoholism. Nonetheless, having read Wilson's letter, Jung felt confident enough in Bill's understanding of the psychospiritual nature of alcoholism to depict it from such an angle, adopting what he called "medieval language" to do so, a clear nod to Meister Eckhart and the other mystics he so admired. Jung explained that it was a tack he refused to take with his patient Rowland: "I am risking it with you [Bill] because I conclude from your very decent and honest letter, that you have acquired a point of view above the misleading platitudes one usually hears about alcoholism."[4] Jung then proceeds to set the journey of the alcoholic within the framework of Western myth—where God and the Devil fight for eternal custody over the souls of alcoholics much as they battled over the fate of the prophet named Job:

> I am strongly convinced that the evil principle prevailing in this world, leads the unrecognized spiritual need into perdition, if it is not counteracted by a real religious insight or by the protective wall of human community. An ordinary man, not protected by an action from above and isolated by society cannot resist the power of evil, which is very aptly called

---

[4]Jung, *Letters*, vol. 2, p. 624.

> the Devil. But the use of such words arouse so
> many mistakes that one can only keep aloof
> from them as much as possible.[5]

This is perhaps the most challenging content of the Wilson letter, impossible to interpret properly outside of Jung's psychological approach. The religious tone of Jung's commentary on the plight of the alcoholic was one Wilson never adopted in his own writings for the same reasons that a psychiatrist would hesitate to employ it with one of his patients. Jung's statement can easily be mistaken to imply that alcoholism stems from a moral deficiency. And yet, Jung's letter is meant to challenge that old trope, still held by "normies" and drunkards alike, who believe that an alcoholic at base lacks either moral fortitude or properly focused self-discipline, or both. Jung salutes the cofounder of Alcoholics Anonymous for "acquiring a point of view above these misleading platitudes," for it allowed him to frankly discuss the disease from the psychological perspective of Western myth.

An Insoluble Dilemma

And while he knew his discussion of the Devil would trigger the religious prejudice of many who read the letter, Jung believed that the function that symbol plays is so paramount in the process of individuation that we avoid it at our own peril. The very fact that our Western spiritual vocabulary lacks

---

[5] Jung, *Letters*, vol. 2, p. 624.

adequate substitutes for the symbol of the Devil is why Jung insisted on using it in his illustration to Wilson, fraught as it is. Relating the alcoholics' battles with their own personal demons to the overarching story told in our Western myths of the cosmogonic conflict between God and the Devil can be tricky even for Twelve Steppers who have adopted a relative view of the God-image and are laboring intensely in an attempt to integrate the shadow. And yet, the most profound, life-changing truth becomes available only after we confront our longest-held prejudices, religious and otherwise.

Jung held that the psychological energy beneath the symbol we call the Devil manifests in the formation of certain pathologies that constellate around a split in the psyche, such as alcoholism and addiction.[6] In the following passage, taken from *Psychological Types*, he begins to unwrap the problem of evil and its relationship to psychopathology:

> Just as the conscious mind can put the question "Why is there this frightful conflict between good and evil?," so the unconscious can reply, "Look closer. Each needs the other. The best, just because it is the best, holds the seeds of evil, and there is nothing so bad but good can come of it."[7]

Similar to the conflict between instinct and spirit, the psychological push and pull between "good" and "evil"

---

[6] Jung writes that "in the Middle Ages … they spoke of the devil, [but] today we call it a neurosis." Jung, *CW*, vol. 10, para. 309.
[7] Jung, *CW*, vol. 6, para. 289.

represents an *insoluble dilemma*, meaning that at a certain point it can only be answered by the antithetical energies emanating from the unconscious. Jung explains that the unconscious will first "respond" to such a quandary with a compensatory image, in a dream or a myth, with which to help the psyche move toward an integration of the opposites. However, in certain cases where the tension becomes more heightened, the unconscious may "take the lead" (rather than just "respond," he says), whipping up a neurosis that aids in waking one up from their state of spiritual antipathy: "Thanks to the neurosis contrived by the unconscious, they are shaken out of their apathy, and this in spite of their own laziness and often desperate resistance."[8] And while psychopathology can actually help to open the door to a middle way, Jung says that, unfortunately, most of us are unwilling to push up against the limits of our mental and moral fortitude: "Despite their notorious unconsciousness, [most people] never get anywhere near a neurosis."[9]

Ironically, Jung refers to those for whom such a troubled state does develop as "higher types," people whose "nature does not in the long run persist in what is for them an unnatural torpor ... bit by bit [energy] accumulates in the unconscious and finally explodes in the form of a more or less acute neurosis."[10] In the case of alcoholics and drug addicts, Twelve Step experience tells us that they are people who, as a rule, find it unbearable to exist without a functioning and

---

[8] Jung, *CW*, vol. 6, para. 290.
[9] Jung, *CW*, vol. 6, para. 291.
[10] Jung, *CW*, vol. 6, para. 291.

reliable set of mythological symbols with which to contain the emergent energies of the unconscious. Wilson describes them as people who are "handicapped by obstinacy, sensitiveness, and unreasoning prejudice" toward spiritual ideas, who feel every conflict intensely—reminiscent of the insoluble tension of opposites they can sense brewing within as much as without our souls. And in a desperate search for a resolution, they turn their spiritual gaze toward "drinking and drugging," finding in it a way to at least temporarily escape. For alcoholics, their dedication to spirits eventuates an acute neurosis, the solution to which demands "the recognition and unavoidable integration of the shadow."[11] Thus, alcohol*ism* creates the perfect setup for a person to stumble upon the path to wholeness, as the need to keep the primordial energies of the unconscious bottled up becomes paramount not just for one's continued sense of well-being, but for one's very survival.

A strong case could be made, based on how wide-spread the disease is coupled with how common Twelve Step recovery has become, that alcoholism is among the most potent of modern means capable of igniting a quest for enlightenment, as it taps directly into the dark, archaic urges of the unconscious, the root of profound spiritual energy. Jung says that it's impossible to determine whether the unconscious is "striving to realize certain definite ends," though he admits that when it comes to certain psychopathologies there is evidence to support the claim that they in fact do evince "an urge towards self-realization."[12] Alcoholism in particular

---

[11] Jung, *CW*, vol. 9i, para. 487.
[12] Jung, *CW*, vol. 6, para. 291.

fulfills just such *an urge*, and we might even go so far as to guess that this unique form of mental and spiritual illness has been derived by the Universal Mind in response to the West's mythlessness as a means to bring about an expansion of spiritual consciousness for the collective, who is in dire need of a new myth. And while such a postulate might seem a stretch, it's worthy of note that as a means of human transformation, alcoholism represents a double-edged sword, razor sharp on both sides: The neurosis punctures the ego, bringing about the prerequisite psychospiritual death, and the accompanying archetypal image of wholeness (*the Alcoholic*) aids the ego in integrating the supraordinate, polaristic powers it has encountered in the psyche.

Self-annihilation

Joseph Campbell, in *The Hero with a Thousand Faces*, helps us to further unravel the complex role the Evil One plays in our quest for metamorphosis by drawing upon the imagery of otherworldly beasts that surround the entrances of ancient and modern temples and sacred spaces of religions across the globe. We see again in his description how the encounter with darkness is a prerequisite to spiritual rebirth. These devilish creatures' relationship to the Presence inside the temple reflect the nature of the antithetical play, depicted in Western myth, between the powers of good and evil. Campbell describes the journey toward the temple doors and interior, lined by beasts with sharp claws, drawn swords, and exposed teeth, as similar to the passage through the jaws of the whale en route to the darkness of its belly:

[The passage into the belly of the whale] gives emphasis to the lesson that the passage of the threshold [into the temple] is a form of self-annihilation. ... But here, instead of passing outward, beyond the confines of the visible world, the hero goes inward, to be born again. The disappearance corresponds to the passing of a worshiper into the temple—where he is to be quickened by the recollection of who and what he is, namely dust and ashes unless immortal. The temple interior, the belly of the whale, and the heavenly land beyond, above, and below the confines of the world, are one and the same. That is why the approaches of and the entrances to temples are flanked and defended by colossal gargoyles: dragons, lions, devil-slayers with drawn swords, resentful dwarves, winged bulls. These are the threshold guardians to ward away all incapable of encountering the higher silence within. They are preliminary embodiments of the dangerous aspect of the presence, corresponding to the mythological ogres that bound the conventional world, or to the two rows of teeth of the whale. They illustrate the fact that the devotee at the moment of the entry into the temple undergoes a metamorphosis. His secular character remains without; he sheds it as a snake its slough. Once inside he may be said to have died to time and returned to the World Womb, the World Navel, the Earthly Paradise. The mere fact that anyone can physically walk past the temple guardians does not invalidate their significance; for if the intruder is incapable of encompassing the sanctuary, he has effectually remained without. Anyone unable to understand a god sees it as a devil and is thus defended from the approach. Allegorically, then, the passage into a temple and the hero-dive through the jaws of the whale are identical adventures, both denoting, in the picture language, the life-centering, life-renewing act.[13]

Campbell's description illustrates the psychological role of evil in an alcoholic's metamorphosis, which really begins with a spiritual death, or the collapse of the ego. That is why Campbell calls "the hero-dive into the temple" a form of "self-annihilation"; passing into any new spiritual landscape requires a prior shift in perception, without which the entrant "effectually remains without." Such a death is symbolic of a change in attitude which only comes about through a rather violent psychological ordeal, resulting in the death of the old self. Campbell quotes Ananda Coomaraswamy, among the first of the sages to bring Eastern religious culture to the West, on the prerequisite for entering into a more enlightened state of consciousness: "No creature can attain a higher grade of nature without ceasing to exist."[14] In the world of the psyche,

---

[13] Joseph Campbell, *The Hero with a Thousand Faces*, 3rd ed, Bollingen Series XVII (Novato, Calif: New World Library, 2008), p. 77. Hereafter *Hero*.
[14] Cited in Campbell, *Hero*, 77.

as in nature, death always precedes rebirth and life, and in the alcoholic mythos, the devils who guard the entrance depict the severing of one's "self-reliance"[15]—hence their drawn swords, open mouths, and exposed teeth—ready and able to cut, gnaw, and tear the ego apart—inducing the ego's death prior to its rebirth into a world of expanding consciousness.

In the Twelve Step myth, the greeters who stand outside the doors of meeting halls, hoping to make the newcomer feel welcome, have been cast in a similar, sacred role as Campbell's temple guardians represent.[16] For, in the psyche of practically every alcoholic wandering up to their first meeting, often still reeking of booze and smarting with "a bad case of the jitters,"[17] the greeters embody a far more numinous presence than what we associate with just a friendly face and a warm welcome: In the mind of the newcomer, they might as well be growling lions or menacing gargoyles, ready to cut down anyone unworthy to pass, providing an early test of the alcoholic's willingness, the extent of the "desire to stop drinking."[18] A similar correlation can be drawn from the Old Testament myth of Eden: When Adam and Eve were forced out of the Garden due to their partaking of the forbidden fruit (a symbol of spiritual death effected by the devilish serpent), God placed cherubim and a flaming sword to "guard" the gate's entrance, lest the two disobedient children sneak back

---

[15] *Alcoholics Anonymous*, 68.
[16] *Sacred* means "to sacrifice with the purpose of making holy," i.e., to induce a spiritual death. Similarly, to sacrifice means to "make holy."
[17] *Alcoholics Anonymous*, 32.
[18] Tradition three states that "the only requirement for membership is a desire to stop drinking." *Alcoholics Anonymous*, 562.

into the garden and unworthily partake of the fruit of the Tree of Life. That flaming sword is a cutting tool imbued with numinosity representative of the self-annihilation required before one can enter the higher silence within, and like the bottle in the mythos of *the Alcoholic* is the metaphorical weapon that brings about the death of our secular character. Wilson calls this cutting action, "getting rid of self,"[19] the killing of the ego's false pretense of its own power and control. As newcomers approach the greeters en route to their first meeting, too full of shame to look *anyone* in the eye, crossing the threshold they "die to time and return to the World Navel, entering into an Earthly Paradise." The fact that they make it through the door and into their first AA meeting suggests that something of profound significance has been left outside—the belief that they "would somehow, someday learn to control and enjoy their drinking." Once inside, the unbelievable tales of the modern shamans will continue to cut away at the dross of the psyche, carving out enough "space between their ears" for the lifesaving medicine to enter.

The demons that alcoholics encounter, behind their compulsion to imbibe, are what prepares them to enter the holy of holies—evocative of the journey into the depths of the psyche where they are destined to uncover a unique conception of a power greater than ourselves. Campbell helps to clarify the psychological function of evil on the path to enlightenment when he says that "anyone unable to understand a god sees it as a devil and is thus defended from the approach." The energy embodied by the beasts

---

[19] *Alcoholics Anonymous*, 66.

occupying the temple grounds corresponds to the energy that we encounter inside—the numinosum, in its positive and negative aspects. Real and lasting transformative work must include both sides of the good/evil dilemma—God and the Devil must both be conceived as psychological functions, both recognized as powers greater than the ego. Just as we must learn to comprehend our own divinity in order to pass into a higher state of consciousness, we must also learn to integrate the evil that lurks within. That's why Jung could so confidently proclaim, "I am indeed convinced that evil is as positive a factor as good."[20] In terms of the Twelve Steps, the dark powers that the Devil represents are constellated within the ism of alcohol, and if alcoholics fail to fully embrace all of themselves, good and bad, they will not experience "an entire psychic change."

Thus, the Devil and his evil power is indicative of many things, not the least of which is our overarching instinct for ease and comfort, the desires of the flesh that, when faithfully followed to their bittersweet ends, induce the necessary spiritual severing. *Gods* and *devils* are nothing more than masks that the numinosum adorns in its interactions with the ego as we make our way toward the threshold—the same antimonial energy reflected by the Trickster and *the Alcoholic*—illustrative of the coupling of our highest religious experience with our most depraved state of being. So while it appears to the uninitiated that the devilish beasts outside the temple were placed there by the Presence within to keep the immoral and unworthy from passing, (the way we had

---

[20] Jung, *CW*, vol. 11, para. 1592.

assumed Yahweh used the flaming sword to "guard the way of the Tree of Life"),[21] those who integrate their darkness are able see the Devil-image from a completely different perspective, that of the objective psyche, which reveals the Devil to be a spirit guide who, through a devious plan gave them the spiritual momentum needed to finally burst through the temple door, "to come all the way in and sit all the way down" as the greeters encourage the newcomer to do. The dilemma of good versus evil is reflective of either side of the transcendent function in the psyche, and Campbell observes, "If a person is able to absorb and integrate [each of them], there will be an almost superhuman degree of self-consciousness and masterful control."[22]

Thus, the evils that drive us toward the temple door are what prepare us for the immense power and glory that awaits beyond the threshold. Those still outside, who have yet to reckon with the evil of their own nature, believe it is the Devil who keeps them out, but those who have made it through did so by learning to recognize the Devil as nothing more than one of the many masks of God and, paradoxically, the bringer of the greatest blessing they could have ever been given—the collapse of the ego at depth—the spiritual death that is translated in the Twelve Step meetings as "G.O.D., the gift of desperation." In the end, we come to recognize that it was the Devil who first unlocked the transformative powers of the Universal Mind, preparing us for "the awful event of the meeting [with the numinosum]" taking place inside.[23]

---

[21] Genesis 3:22, 24.

[22] Campbell, *Hero*, 53.

[23] Cited in Campbell, *Oriental Mythology*, 46.

13

The Christ-image

Understanding the psychological basis of the problem of opposites in Western myth is helpful in our quest to integrate our lowest and highest aspects as we try and harness the transformative energy of the numinosum. Such a synthesis is often referred to as a state of *wholeness*, a term the Oxford dictionary defines as "complete and harmonious; being unbroken or undamaged."[1] Psychologically speaking, wholeness equates to the integration of "all of us, good and bad,"[2] thus diverging from the typical religious notions of *salvation* or *redemption* that we're used to. The Twelve Step myth alludes to wholeness, most notably in Step Two as our "restoration to sanity." When Jung described Rowland's insatiable craving for liquor as evidence of an intangible thirst for wholeness, he meant to say that our longing for wholeness is buried within our shadow complexes, such as alcoholism or addiction. But in order to achieve wholeness, we have to deal with our shadow in a way that Western culture (including religion) is unable to facilitate, having become fixated on just

---

[1] Charles T. Onions, ed. *The Oxford Dictionary of English Etymology* (Reprinted Oxford: Oxford Univ. Press, 1996).
[2] *Alcoholics Anonymous*, 76.

the "good" side of the cosmic equation, turning a blind eye to the accompanying dark and corrupted one.

In the Christian interpretation, for instance, salvation hinges on the sacrifice of Christ, who was "perfect." And while the Christ symbol plays an important role in the Western psyche, none of us will ever come close to attaining perfection the way he did (in the metaphysical sense).[3] In Christian dogma, Christ had to be perfect in order to expiate sin and thereby appease the wrath of Yahweh, which he did in the form of his own sacrifice, the Atonement, wherein he suffered greatly, taking up the cross on our behalf. After this selfless act, Christ was resurrected and thus saved all of God's creation from the awful fate of sin and death ushered in by the Fall of Adam and Eve. In the end of time, Christ's enemy, the Devil, will be cast into "outer darkness" for eternity, and the power of evil will be stamped out for good. Such is the doctrine of Christian salvation, in a nutshell.

An Incomplete God-image

On the surface, it appears that Western theology accounts for both sides of the cosmic conflict between good and evil. However, examining the Christian myth from an analytical perspective led Jung to conclude that conventional Western religion does not accurately reflect the psychospiritual process required for wholeness, which necessitates the

---

[3] Wilson also lets his readers off the hook: "We are not saints. The point is, that we are willing to grow along spiritual lines. The principles we have set down are guides to progress. We claim spiritual progress rather than spiritual perfection." (*Alcoholics Anonymous*, 60).

acceptance and integration of the dark side of our being as well as the light. The fact that the Christ-image has been left entirely devoid of darkness troubled Jung, who reasoned that a religious image lacking both sides of the good/evil polarity equally is *incomplete*.[4] Sure, the Christ-figure illuminates certain aspects of our spiritual journey, but we don't have the luxury of casting away evil with the mere mandate, "Get thee hence, Satan!" the way he did.[5] For all humans, but especially alcoholics and addicts, quite the opposite is true—the more we try to avoid the power of evil, the stronger its influence becomes, evidenced by the fact that our "countless vain attempts to prove we could drink like other people"[6] inevitably made matters worse. And while Christian dogma teaches that Christ's spotlessness allowed him to atone for our sins, making perfection the end-all-be-all of salvation has conditioned us to turn a blind eye to our own dark and evil nature—to sweep our shadow under the rug—compounding the spiritual crisis so evident throughout the world today. As we had to learn "in the rooms," the shadow can only be ignored for so long before it makes itself known in ways that are absolutely terrifying to an unsuspecting ego.

Thus, one of the most penetrating insights we can glean into our individual psychospiritual development is that

[4] This helps to explain why so many in dire need of a spiritual transformation, who have been driven by an archaic component within the psyche to sacrifice the last ounce of our mental and moral character upon its shrines, have been unable to rely upon a traditional interpretation of the Western God-image in a meaningful way.
[5] See Matthew 4:10.
[6] *Alcoholics Anonymous*, 30.

our conception of religious images mirrors our relationship to our own darkness. In *Aion* (*Volume 9ii* of the *Collected Works,* published in 1951), Jung taught that the exclusion of the shadow from the conventional God-image of the West has become a rather formidable roadblock on the path to enlightenment: "The Christ-symbol lacks wholeness in the modern psychological sense since it does not include the dark side of things but specifically excludes it in the form of a Luciferian opponent."[7] To make matters worse, the men who formulated Christian dogma sought to minimize Lucifer's influence through a doctrine called the *privato boni,* which states that evil is merely the absence of good. This doctrine didn't please Jung at all, who, like many of us in recovery, was well aware of the dark and compulsive nature of the psyche and how much power it actually wields: "If Christian metaphysics clings to the *privato boni*, it is giving expression to the tendency always to increase the good and diminish the bad."[8] Over the course of centuries, the ideology composed by the Church fathers imbued the God-image with more and more impeccability while at the same time attempted to subdue Satan's influence in the cosmos, going so far as to define evil as merely "the accidental lack of perfection."[9]

---

[7] Jung, *CW*, vol. 9ii, para. 74.

[8] Jung, *CW*, vol. 9ii, para. 98. Herrmann mentions, on page 49 of *Doorways to the Self*, that Jung was "most interested in understanding ... the nature of evil in humans."

[9] Jung, *CW*, vol. 9ii, para. 74.

Enantiodromia

Like alcoholics who insist they don't have a drinking problem but have bottles of booze hidden all over the house, the Church fathers imagined they could ditch the burden of evil by the wayside in their quest for spiritual mountaintops, unable to foresee that in doing so, they would inadvertently usher in the "anti-Christian" world we live in today, due to a macrocosmic psychological backlash to their specious reasoning:

> The ideal of spirituality striving for the heights was doomed to clash with the materialistic earth-bound passion to conquer matter and master the world. ... The subsequent developments ... can only be called "anti-christian" in a sense that confirms the early Christian anticipation of the "end of time." It is as if, with the coming of Christ, opposites that were latent till then had become manifest, or as if a pendulum had swung violently to one side and were now carrying out the complementary movement in the opposite direction. No tree, it is said, can grow to heaven unless its roots reach down to hell. The double meaning of this movement lies in the nature of the pendulum.[10]

The Church's insistence on a theophany that honors only one side of the cosmic equation initiated a collective psychological

---

[10] Jung, CW, vol. 9ii, para. 78.

reaction whereby utter evil and darkness were unleashed into the world, ushering in the thousand-year reign of terror prophesied in the Book of Revelation, which continues to escalate today.

In a similar finding in the realm of the physical sciences, physicists discovered that subatomic particle pairs are so intimately connected that when one of them flips over to its opposite, the other of the pair (which might be anywhere else in the universe) also flips *at the exact same moment*, perhaps in defiance of the natural laws of time and space. Those same energies exist in the human psyche, where they show a similar propensity, and when the symbol depicting the power of evil was cut-off from consciousness, it triggered a reversal within the collective psychology whereby darkness was stirred in equal measure and, much like a psychopathology may erupt in the life of an individual who has become unconsciously captivated by one side of a crisis of opposites, a similar situation evolved for Western consciousness in general, leading to the worldwide spiritual pandemic that would become the catalyst for modern alcoholism and addiction. The following statement from *Aion* explains how this powerful dynamic works:

> Psychologically the case is clear, since the dogmatic figure of Christ is so sublime and spotless that everything else turns dark beside it. It is, in fact, so one-sidedly perfect that it demands a psychic complement to restore the balance. ... The coming of the Antichrist is not just a prophetic prediction—it is an inexorable psychological law whose existence, though

unknown to the author of the Johannine Epistles, brought him a sure knowledge of the impending enantiodromia. Consequently he wrote as if he were conscious of the inner necessity for this transformation, though we may be sure that the idea seemed to him like a divine revelation. In reality every intensified differentiation of the Christ-image brings about a corresponding accentuation of its unconscious complement, thereby increasing the tension between above and below. In making these statements we are keeping entirely within the sphere of Christian psychology and symbolism. A factor that no one has reckoned with, however, is the fatality inherent in the Christian disposition itself, which leads inevitably to a reversal of its spirit—not through the obscure workings of chance but in accordance with psychological law.[11]

Here Jung tells us that the Church's miscalculation in diminishing the Devil's role would turn out to be a costly mistake for Christianity, signaling the end of its spiritual vitality. Curtailing the symbol of darkness did the exact opposite of what the Church fathers intended, leaving the world dangerously exposed to the primordial powers being unleashed from within the collective unconscious. Jung coined the term *enantiodromia* to describe the tendency

---

[11] Jung, *CW*, vol. 9ii, paras. 77-78.

of things to dramatically change into their opposite—"to run the other way" or to "swing violently in the opposite direction," like a pendulum in motion.[12] Assuming the Universal Mind permeates everything in existence, then the same enantiodromic tendencies that exist on the macro scale (in nature, in the body, and in space) can also be discovered emanating from the microcosm that makes up the human soul. Thus, the coincidence of opposites that manifests as quantum entanglement in physis shows up as an "inexorable psychological law" as well, leading to a "reversal of spirit" in both the individual as well as the collective psyche.

The Boy Whistling in the Dark

The enantiodromia that so greatly affects Western culture through the faulty interpretation of our religious symbols affects all of us. Anytime a person unconsciously identifies with only one side of a psychological antinomy—an *ism*—the side they turn away from increases in intensity. We see a similar situation play out ever so clearly in the mythos of the Anonymous Alcoholic, who has "[sworn] off forever with and without a solemn oath,"[13] not unlike how the Church fathers imagined that by diminishing the symbol of evil, they could abolish its effects. In the fellowships, such a spiritual blind spot is called "whistling in the dark," taken from the following instructive passage in the Big Book regarding the alcoholic's relationship to that *magic elixir*:

---

[12] Joseph Campbell and David Kudler, *Pathways to Bliss: Mythology and Personal Transformation* (Novato, Calif: New World Library, 2004), pp. 64-65.
[13] *Alcoholics Anonymous*, 31.

Now and then a serious drinker, being dry at the moment says, "I don't miss it at all. Feel better. Work better. Having a better time." As ex-problem drinkers, we smile at such a sally. We know our friend is like a boy whistling in the dark to keep up his spirits. He fools himself. Inwardly he would give anything to take half a dozen drinks and get away with them. He will presently try the old game again, for he isn't happy about his sobriety. He cannot picture life without alcohol. Some day he will be unable to imagine life either with alcohol or without it. Then he will know loneliness such as few do. He will be at the jumping-off place. He will wish for the end.[14]

The boy whistling in the dark is among the shadow figures Bill unwittingly formulated in the Big Book, representative of a certain attitude of the Anonymous Alcoholic at an early stage of his "drinking career"[15] when he is unconsciously identified with the archetype of *the Alcoholic*. For active alcoholics, life without spirits is inconceivable, but a truly impossible dilemma arises when they can no longer imagine life with it either— the moment of metanoia, when the opposites of the *spiritus contra spiritum* paradox are activated and another, far more dangerous shadow character of Wilson's making takes center

---

[14] *Alcoholics Anonymous*, 151-152.
[15] *Alcoholics Anonymous*, 30.

stage: "King Alcohol,"[16] who once donned the regal robes of *Spiritus,* suddenly morphs into *spiritum* and, grabbing them by the throat, begins to choke out their spirit. Paradoxically, rather than coaxing them to make the decision to give up drinking— *which doesn't work for the kind of alcoholic Wilson describes throughout the Big Book*—in order to release the hold that alcohol has on them, alcoholics must "fully surrender to it," accepting the ugly fact that, even with the help of AA, they are unlikely to "stay stopped," that the best hope they have is for "a daily reprieve contingent upon the maintenance of [their] spiritual condition."[17]

Ironically, when alcoholics arrive at such a "seemingly hopeless state of mind and body,"[18] they have finally stumbled upon the only attitude that might actually lead to a long-term solution. Wilson explains, "We had to fully concede to our innermost selves that we were alcoholics. This is the first step in recovery. The delusion that we are like other people, or presently may be, has to be smashed."[19] Since the psyche always tends toward enantiodromia, those who still think their "firm resolution not to drink again"[20] is sufficient to keep them sober will probably be drunk in short order. On the flip side, the minute they surrender to the idea that they are powerless over alcohol and are therefore likely to drink again "no matter what" is the very minute they might actually solve what has become an insoluble psychological dilemma.

---

[16] *Alcoholics Anonymous*, 151.

[17] *Alcoholics Anonymous*, 85.

[18] *Alcoholics Anonymous*, 20.

[19] *Alcoholics Anonymous*, 30.

[20] *Alcoholics Anonymous*, xxix.

Jung explains how this phenomenon works: "Completeness is forced upon us against all our conscious strivings."[21] Meaning that giving up the fight against the drink is far more effective at bringing about a fundamental change in one's relationship to alcohol than all one's conscious efforts to avoid it.

Thus, the mythos of *the Alcoholic* clarifies how the enantiodromic tendencies of the psyche propel us toward transformation, compelling us to find a way through the middle of our psychological conflicts by fully surrendering to the darkness that is inherent within our own being. Sadly, alcoholics who are still caught in the mental trap of "whistling in the dark" will not be able to stave off relapse much longer. Deep down, in a place they probably don't even know exists, they would "give anything to have a couple of drinks, and get away with it," exhibiting the same attitude as the Church fathers, who had fooled themselves into thinking that by shackling the Devil to their dogma, they could somehow help the Almighty *Czar of Heaven* inspire more good in the world.

---

[21] Jung, *CW*, vol. 9ii, par. 123.

Part Four

The Ego and the Self

14

The Self

After the conference at Clark University in 1909, during the years leading up to the discovery of his *personal myth* in Taos and Africa, Jung embarked upon an in-depth examination of the Upanishads, comparing it with the writings of William James and Meister Eckhart, his two most beloved gurus. Already keenly familiar with the problem of opposites that permeates the human condition, the lack of wholeness in the Western God-image prompted Jung to reimagine the higher power just as Bill Wilson did following his own spiritual trajectory. Steven Herrmann points out in *Doorways to the Self* that Jung could sense "the birth of a new God-concept"[1] brewing in the Western psyche, an image of which emerged out of his "simultaneous reading of the Upanishads, Eckhart, and James."[2] Jung longed for a conception of God that could contain the powerful energies emanating from the unconscious, *a suitable symbol of the fusion of the pairs of opposites that might empower him to function in*

---

[1] Herrmann, *Doorways*, 155.
[2] Herrmann writes that "The Self is a transpersonal notion that evolved from Jung's simultaneous reading of the Upanishads, Eckhart, and James." *Doorways*, 194.

society without shutting out the primitive—just as he would encourage Jaime to seek a short time later. By the time Jung met Jaime, he had already introduced just such a notion in his *Two Essays on Analytical Psychology* published in 1917, now volume 7 of his *Collected Works*. Herrmann tells us that Jung felt inspired to introduce a figure that would unite the Eastern conception of divinity (*Brahman, the breath of life*) with the relative God-image that his intellectual heroes had cultivated (William James and Meister Eckhart, who led him to *Spiritus*, or *the breath of life*), and he decided to name it *the Self.*

Unlike a conventional notion of the Western deity, the Self is an image of wholeness and as such presupposes a conjunction of the opposites. In *Aion*, where Jung more fully fleshed out the concept of the Self, he writes, "In the empirical self, light and shadow form a paradoxical unity [while] in the Christian concept, on the other hand, the archetype is hopelessly split into two. ... [Wholeness] is the birth of the self."[3] An expression of the same primordial energies that make up *the Alcoholic* archetype, the Self is a fundamental psychological construct—a cornerstone upon which human consciousness rests. A personification of the collective unconscious, the Self sits opposite the ego, which Jung tells us is the "point of reference for the field of consciousness," explaining that we are aware of things "only as far as they are related to the ego" since "the ego is the subject of all personal

---

[3] Jung, *CW*, vol. 9ii, paras. 76, 550. Note that Jung does not capitalize the word "self" in his own works, but the tradition since Jung has been to capitalize the term (as "Self") in order to distinguish it from the more common usage of "self" in everyday language.

acts of consciousness."[4] The ego is thus the mechanism in the human psyche through which we relate to *everything* we are conscious of, making up our "subjective identity."[5]

The dynamic taking place between the ego and Self forms the psychological basis of all Western myth, including the Twelve Steps. From such a perspective, the human characters typify the ego, the carrier of consciousness, and whenever the symbol of God is present, it is representative of the Self—the *central* autonomous psychic complex. The ego extends as far as the limits of one's individual consciousness, but the Self "comprises the totality of the psyche,"[6] so it includes both the conscious and the unconscious. Thus, the part of the Self that is conscious is called *ego*, but the Self extends well beyond the horizon of consciousness, incorporating the individual shadow and from there reaching into the unfathomable depths of the collective unconscious. Therefore, the Self encompasses the ego and yet remains almost entirely unknown and unknowable: As such, the Self is a power greater than the ego, "indistinguishable" from the God-image in myth.[7]

The Inflated Ego

At base, the psychic change we seek through spiritual transformation represents a shift in the way the conscious ego

---

[4] Jung, *CW*, vol. 9ii, paras. 2-3, 11.
[5] See Edinger, *Ego and Archetype*, 3. The Self may also be referred to as "the objective psyche," contrasted with the ego as one's "subjective identity."
[6] Jung, *CW*, vol. 9ii, par. 717.
[7] Jung, *CW*, vol. 11, para. 233.

relates to the unconscious, supraordinate Self. When we're born, we don't have an ego; it grows out of the Self as we come of age. Edward Edinger explained that "in earliest infancy, no ego or consciousness exists. All is in the unconscious. The latent ego is in complete identification with the Self. The Self is born, but the ego is made; and in the beginning all is Self."[8] As the ego emerges, it naturally identifies as being one with the Self, the way an infant relates to its mother. An ego that unconsciously identifies with the Self is called an "inflated ego," a state that persists into adulthood, *especially among alcoholics and addicts*. Edinger writes that for the inflated ego, its "total being and experience are ordered around the a priori assumption of a deity."[9] An ego that is still identified with the Self believes that it is both all-knowing and all-powerful, "the smartest person in the room," as we hear in Twelve Step meetings. Bill Wilson intuited a similar problem for the alcoholic ego, writing that "we had to quit playing God—it didn't work."[10] Wilson recognized that

> most people live by self-propulsion. Each person is like an actor who wants to run the whole show; is forever trying to arrange the lights, the ballet, the scenery and the rest of the players in his own way. If his arrangements would only stay put, if only people would do as he wished, the show would be great. Everybody,

---

[8] Edinger, *Ego and Archetype*, 7.
[9] Edinger, *Ego and Archetype*, 7.
[10] *Alcoholics Anonymous*, 62.

including himself, would be pleased. Life would
be wonderful.[11]

Indeed, whenever we find ourselves attempting to control any
person, place, or thing, we act from an "a priori assumption of
a deity." Wilson goes on to explain that the alcoholic especially
is "a victim of the delusion that he can wrest satisfaction and
happiness out of this world if he only manages well."[12] The
delusion of control one experiences with regards to alcohol or
drugs epitomizes every inflated ego that feigns more influence
than it actually has. Deep down, all of us secretly assume
that our savvy alone makes us best equipped to manage the
outcome of every situation—yours or mine—when in reality,
the ego has very little sway over much of anything in life, often
unable to control even the very next thought or action. Jung
says the ego is "driven to act yet free to reflect."[13] It is the
unconscious Self, the "inner empirical deity,"[14] who is actually
running the show—all the ego can do is reflect upon and
bravely accept that fact, as suggested in the first three steps.

And while the inflationary attitude that Wilson
describes is heightened in people with alcoholic tendencies,
no one is exempt from experiencing it from time to time:
Periods of inflation and deflation are part of the alternating
natural cycle of spiritual death and rebirth taking place in
every moment of every human life. Edinger, who addressed
a crowd far removed from the alcoholics that comprise

---

[11] *Alcoholics Anonymous*, 60.
[12] *Alcoholics Anonymous*, 62.
[13] Jung, *CW*, vol. 8, para. 406.
[14] Edinger, *Ego and Archetype*, 3.

Wilson's readership, nevertheless uses very similar language to describe the inflated ego:

> There are numerous examples of inflation, which we might call the inflation of everyday life. We can identify a state of inflation when-ever we see someone (including ourselves) living out an attitude of deity, i.e., whenever one is transcending proper human limits. Spells of anger are examples of inflated states. The attempt to force and coerce one's environment is the predominant motivation in anger. It is a kind of Yahweh complex. The urge to vengeance is also identification with deity. At such times, one might recall the injunction, "Vengeance is mine' saith the Lord" i.e., "not yours."
>
> Power motivations of all kinds are symptomatic of inflation. Whenever one operates out of a power motive, omnipotence is implied. But omnipotence is an attribute only of God. Intellectual rigidity which attempts to equate its own private truth or opinion with universal truth is also inflation. It is the assumption of omniscience. Lust and all operations of the pure pleasure principle are likewise inflation. Any desire that considers its own fulfillment the central value transcends the reality limits of the ego and hence is assuming attributes of transpersonal powers.

> Practically all of us, deep down, have a residue of inflation that is manifested as immortality. There is scarcely anyone that is thoroughly and totally disidentified with this aspect of inflation. ...Taking on oneself too much of anything is [also] indicative of inflation because it transcends proper human limits. Too much humility as well as too much arrogance, too much love and altruism as well as too much power striving and selfishness, are all symptoms of inflation.[15]

Though it is possible to achieve freedom from ego-inflation intermittently, we will never fully outgrow it. For no matter how far up (or down) the road of individuation we've traveled, we are constantly threatened with slipping back into unconscious identification with the Self, when our ego tries to run the show. Whether we practice the Twelve Steps or follow some other spiritual discipline, the trick is to cultivate awareness of our unconscious attempts at "playing God," and, as the saying in the fellowships goes, to "turn it over" as quickly as possible. Doing so, we learn to see that bouts of inflation are whisperings from the unconscious Self that we've become unplugged from our Source, thus opening up passageways into the Unconscious Mind meant to enhance our spiritual aptitude.

---

[15] Edinger, *Ego and Archetype*, 14-15.

Expanding Spiritual Consciousness

As the center of the field of consciousness, the ego filters our perception of the world, acting and reacting on the stage of life, unaware that the Self, the "inner empirical deity," is the producer, director, playwright, and audience of the drama that we are forever caught up in. William James recognized this "higher order of things" as well, explaining that a religious attitude "consists of the belief that there is an unseen order and that our supreme good lies in harmoniously adjusting ourselves thereto."[16] The process of Self-realization involves the ego learning to recognize that this "unseen order" stems from an unknown, transcendent aspect of one's own psyche, distinct from itself. In order for the ego to properly adjust in its relationship to that "inner deity," it must relinquish its delusion of control, or its "assumption of omniscience and omnipotence," coming to realize that a supraordinate, autonomous psychic complex is actually in charge, driving us to think, say, and do things that are beyond our control.

The way we disidentify from the Self is by shining the light of consciousness on the shadowy contents of our psyche—beginning with the unseen compulsions behind what often turns out to be self-destructive behavior. And while such a course of action might sound easy, it's not, for the inflated ego doesn't just decide to "let go" of its pretense of transpersonal power—that goes against every survival mechanism the human psyche has carefully evolved since the dawn of time. The ego has to be thoroughly convinced through a tedious

---

[16] James, *Varieties of Religious Experience*, 20.

process that almost always involves an insoluble psychological dilemma. Thus, the Self methodically deconstructs the ego's delusion of control by leading it into a psychological "trap it cannot spring,"[17] of which the adventure of the Anonymous Alcoholic is a spiritual prototype. Step One depicts the deflation of the ego, the psychospiritual death whereby the ego relinquishes its assumption of omniscience and finally admits it is powerless. Then the Self can start guiding the ego toward greater Self-realization, toward a spiritual rebirth and awakening—symbolized in the remaining 11 Steps.

Wilson's character is useful for understanding ego-inflation and deflation, for the harrowing cycle that alcoholics pass through on their way toward "the rooms" is one that everyone experiences to one degree or another as they grow toward Self-realization. As we all endure an unconscious thirst for union with God, so we all suffer from a delusion of control over something or someone, illustrated by the alcoholic belief that the next drink will be the one that finally makes them feel whole. And just as the drinking career of alcoholics is an integral aspect of the arc of their spiritual journey, leading them to the wellspring of life, all of our unconscious reactions (triggered by our assumptions of omniscience) represent doorways that open directly into the unconscious, setting us on the path to enlightenment. If we're lucky, we'll recognize, with Wilson that "Lack of power ... was our dilemma. We had to find a power by which we could live, and it had to be *a Power greater than ourselves*. Obviously. But where and how were we

---

[17] Clancy I. often used the phrase "trap we cannot spring."

to find this Power?"[18] In reality, that most important question itself represents an insoluble dilemma, for the answer lies beyond the ego's grasp. A dilemma that is so confounding that it can awaken the ego from its state of unconscious inflation will require the Self, who authored it, to solve. That's why they say in Twelve Step meetings, unironically, that "our best thinking got us here." Working the Twelve Steps, individuals quickly learn that the process they have embarked upon is designed to "right size the ego." In Jungian terms, the Steps help to realign the ego in its relationship to the Self, the same process symbolized in every myth but perhaps most brilliantly outlined by Wilson's first three suggestions: "We admitted we were powerless...that our lives had become unmanageable. [We] came to believe that a power greater than ourselves could restore us to sanity. [We] made a decision to turn our will and our lives over to the care of God, as we understood Him."[19]

In the letter Wilson wrote to Jung in January of 1961, he described ego-deflation within the context of his own recovery, telling Jung that his stern warning to Rowland about the hopelessness of his chances for recovery from alcoholism was the very thing that spurred Rowland to seek spiritual help. Wilson commented that he had been given a similar message from Dr. Silkworth, with an equally profound impact, repeating an idea he gleaned from his study in early sobriety of William James's *The Varieties of Religious Experience*: "This book gave me the realization that most conversion experiences,

---

[18] *Alcoholics Anonymous*, 45. Italics in original.
[19] *Alcoholics Anonymous*, 59.

whatever their variety, do have a common denominator of ego collapse at depth. The individual faces an impossible dilemma."[20] And while James never used the phrase "ego-collapse," Wilson, eager student as he was, mined it from the depths of the collective unconscious through his keen spiritual intuition while reading James, going on to develop it quite masterfully in the Big Book—the basis of his own *myth of expanding consciousness.*

Every spiritual journey involves "the tremendous polarity of our nature" railroading us into a situation that can only be solved by "the terrifying experience of a psychic process that ... works [us] rather than [us] it."[21] Wilson spoke to Jung of how pivotal Silkworth's "verdict of hopelessness" was for him in his own process of spiritual regeneration, comparing it to the message Hazard had received from Jung: "To me, this was a shattering blow. Just as Rowland had been made ready for his conversion experience by you, so had my wonderful friend Dr. Silkworth prepared me."[22] Such a shattering blow marks what we call our "moment of clarity," when the ego finally awakens to the reality of the dangerous web fate has laid for it. What is shattered, broken, or cut off is the ego's "heartbreaking obsession that [it will find] some new

---

[20] *Grapevine.* It seems that Wilson might have learned of ego deflation from Dr. Harry Tiebout, a clinical psychiatrist and friend of A.A. who worked with Bill during the 1940's when he started to developed depression. Tiebout published multiple articles regarding the nature of the inflated ego and the need for surrender in recovery from alcoholism, which can be found in the Journal of Studies on Alcohol and Drugs, www.jsad.com.

[21] Jung, *CW*, vol. 11, para. 446.

[22] *Grapevine.*

miracle of control."[23] Wilson's phrase "ego collapse at depth" is what Jungians call "ego deflation"; it is the urge toward Self-realization for those of us who have been truly called by the Self to embark upon such a heroic and dangerous task. The alcoholic ego, in the face of such overwhelming evidence, is particularly prone to experience complete collapse, becoming thoroughly convinced that one's sense of control over much of anything in life is just an illusion. Still, recognizing one's powerlessness, even over alcohol or drugs, is almost as hard as it is for us to sense our intangible thirst for union with God—the ego resists making the connection sometimes until it is too late.

---

[23] *Alcoholics Anonymous*, 151.

15

The Fall and the At-one-ment

The cycle described in Twelve Step meetings, through the *personal adventures of what we used to be like, what happened, and what we are like now* illustrates the same drama that is depicted in every Western myth, which, from the psychological perspective, represents the unfolding of the complex relationship between the ego (consciousness) and the Self (the unconscious)—how the two psychological entities interact in the mysterious realm of *Psyche*. In the last chapter, we examined how the ego naturally overidentifies with the Self, creating a state of inflation that is countered by what Wilson called an "ego collapse at depth." Such a deflation, the spiritual death, is reflected by the death of the hero in most legendary stories. In this chapter, we'll explore how in Western myth, the troublesome circumstances that the Creator forces upon his children are a symbolic parallel to the impossible dilemma that the Self presents for the inflated ego, leading to its collapse.

From the psychological perspective, the role of the Creator symbolizes the empirical Self, while the human characters—like Adam and Eve, Jesus, or the Anonymous Alcoholic—reflect the individual ego, or consciousness.

Edward Edinger, in his book *Ego and Archetype*, examines the dynamic between the ego and the Self, elaborating on the nature of that relationship in myth: "The ego's relation to the Self is a highly problematic one and corresponds very closely to man's relation to his Creator as depicted in religious myth. Indeed the myth can be seen as a symbolic expression of the ego-Self relationship."[1] And while Edinger admits that our relationship to the Creator is highly problematic, even that might be an understatement. Sure, we've long interpreted our religious myths to have a fairytalelike ending, but the reality is much more ominous; every adventure into the mythic world involves certain violent death before the promise of renewal is bestowed: even Jesus's Father, the God he called "Love," in the end demanded his blood. In refusing to limit our understanding of myth to the often glossed-over cultural interpretation, we must acknowledge that there is nary a single religious myth that does not escalate into a violent and bloody mess, reflecting a difficult truth about the dynamic that exists between the ego and the Self. Therefore, it shouldn't surprise us when we find our own attempts at forging an intimate relationship with this supraordinate power difficult, to say the least, for "to make the decision to turn one's life and will over to the care of God" is to willfully submit to the ruthlessness, jealousy, and violence that stem from the depths of the collective unconscious.

---

[1] Edinger, *Ego and Archetype*, 4.

The Fall

The dynamic between the ego and the Self is clearly on display in the two mythological pillars of the West, so fundamental to our psychology they are worthy of an in-depth examination from a psychological perspective: the Fall and the Atonement. Exploring these for insight about the ego/Self relationship, we'll want to set aside any preconceived notions that we have of them, passed down to us through generations of religious dogma.

Standing in the Garden of Eden, the first thing to notice is that each important symbol in the narrative is paired with an opposite: The Father and the snake make up a pair (the text tells us they are both "gods"); Adam and Eve are also opposites (male and female); finally, the tree of life sits in contrast to the tree of the knowledge of good and evil (a symbol of death). Edinger says the story of the Fall "symbolizes the birth of the ego," explaining that "awareness of the opposites [is] the specific feature of consciousness."[2] The ego is the seat of consciousness, so the emergence, or birth, of the ego is correlated to our becoming conscious of the opposites. Psychologically, God the Father and the snake are a reflection of the Self, which always appears as a paradoxical unity; Adam and Eve represent the human ego and its shadow, respectively; and the two trees illustrate the coincidence of opposites required for the ego, or consciousness, to awaken— the tool the Self uses to bring about Self-realization.

---

[2] Edinger, *Ego and Archetype*, 18.

As the story goes, God the Father plants the seed of an insoluble dilemma necessary for consciousness to emerge, reflected by the fruit of the two dichotomous trees. He tells Adam and Eve that so long as they only partake of the fruit of the tree of life, they can stay in the paradisiacal state that defines the Garden.³ On the other hand, the consequence of partaking of the fruit of the tree of knowledge is mortality ("do not eat of the fruit of that tree, for if you do, you will certainly die.") The tree of mortality (or death) is also the tree of consciousness—you can't have one without the other—the lesson being that increased consciousness is accompanied by a spiritual death, a gift from the gods even more precious than eternal life in their presence.

In the beginning, Adam and Eve enjoy life in the Garden, although they wouldn't know it unless and until they experienced "evil." As long as they obey the Father, then they are OK; the text tells us that they remain "unashamed of their nakedness."⁴ Still innocent, the impending conflict has yet to emerge, which the Father makes an inroad for by telling the humans not to partake of the fruit of the tree of knowledge, setting up the *conflict of duty* that is the crux of the story: Only

---

³ In the Garden, the Father gives Adam and Eve two commandments that are fundamentally at odds: First, he tells them that they must "multiply and replenish the earth," meaning that they should procreate; next, he tells them that they should not partake of the forbidden fruit, that it would lead to their mortality and death. The conflict of duty that develops in Eden thus lies in the fact that the humans cannot keep both of these commandments, for without partaking of the fruit of the tree of knowledge of good and evil, they would remain innocent, i.e., immortal and therefore unable to procreate.

⁴ Genesis 2:25.

through disobedience to the will of God can the emerging ego become conscious of itself as a being separate from the Self. If eating the fruit of the tree of knowledge of good and evil is forbidden, then increased consciousness is the original sin. Consequently, consciousness of the opposites, gained by experience of *both*, carries within it the seed of spiritual death, but it also disqualifies one from maintaining the psychic state symbolized by life in the wonderful Garden—unconscious identification with the Creator/Self.

That seed of conflict finally sprouts into a dilemma when Adam and Eve are approached by the other one of "the gods" in the Garden—the dark, animalistic aspect of the antimonial Self, disguised this time as a whispering serpent. The Trickster, in the garb of a snake, promises the couple they can become "like one of us" if they partake of the fruit of the tree of knowledge of good and evil. The tension deepens even more when Eve decides to eat the forbidden fruit while Adam hesitates. Eventually, Adam falls for her charms and partakes as well, whereupon they immediately become "ashamed that they were naked," and hearing the voice of God as he walked in the Garden, run into a thicket of bushes to hide and try to cover themselves with branches and leaves. It is noteworthy that the moment we become conscious of the opposites, the ego emerges, and we start to experience uncomfortable emotions, not the least of which are our feelings of fear and shame.[5]

Discovering the couple hiding in the bushes, the Father asks them, "Who told you that you were naked?" Not

---

[5] Genesis 3:10.

sure how to answer what seems like a trick question, Adam blames Eve for giving him the fruit, while she insists that the snake "beguiled" her into eating it. And yet, what they were perhaps still unable to perceive was the simple truth that no one had told them they were naked; becoming conscious, they instinctively knew. Thus, full of fear, shame, and remorse, the two become like islands in the universe, suddenly finding themselves estranged from God, afraid of their own bodies, and at odds with each other. And while the psychological gap between each of the characters widens as the story develops, the devastating magnitude of the situation the humans find themselves in is made crystal clear when, for having partaken of the fruit of *evil*, God casts them out of his presence, to continue their troubled relationship with him in the fallen, natural world beyond the walled Garden.[6]

Paradoxically, in their newly fallen state and having experienced a spiritual death, Adam and Eve are now qualified to "become like the gods." As a token, the gods slay an animal and present the preserved skins to Adam and Eve, to protect them from the harsh elements and to comfort them as they wander through life estranged from their Creator.[7] Buckskins last for generations, whereas the corpses of the sacrificed animals would decompose back into the earth in a short time, providing nutrients for the trees of the Garden. This rare gift from the gods not only marks the advent of mortality; it symbolizes the regenerative cycle of spiritual death and rebirth that the humans must pass through in order to "become like

---

[6] See Genesis 3:22-24.
[7] Genesis 3:21.

the gods." God sets two angels to guard the gate and puts the weapon used to slay the animal—the flaming sword—in their care, the message being that the humans will not be able to reenter the Garden, psychologically speaking, until that "paradoxical knife-edge" is turned upon them, and they undergo the metamorphosis tokenized by the slain animal. As a reflection of the power of the numinosum, the sword cuts away our preconceived notions of what the opposites in the Garden mean, mysteriously conjoining our conceptions of "good and evil" as we begin to discover the paradoxical Self within. Jung says that "the Self is made manifest in the opposites and in the conflict between them; it is a *coincidentia oppositorum*. Hence, the way to the Self begins with conflict."[8]

The Mythos of the Anonymous Alcoholic

Every spiritual adventure follows the same trajectory that develops in Eden, emerging out of an insoluble conflict in the psyche, and the story of the Anonymous Alcoholic helps to elucidate the process of expanding consciousness and the role that the opposing states of good and evil play in the quest for enlightenment. Jung has said, "Without thorough knowledge of 'good and evil,' ego and shadow, there is no recognition of the self."[9] An alcoholic's relationship to alcohol, like the fruit of the tree of knowledge of good and evil, holds the seeds of an ever-deepening conflict from which a higher consciousness may sprout. In the Garden of Eden,

---

[8] Jung, *CW*, vol. 12, para. 259.
[9] Jung, *Letters*, vol. 2, p. 154.

the unconscious Self, in the form of the gods, sets in motion a quandary that engenders the progressive differentiation of the conscious ego, forcing Adam and Eve into a higher state of awareness. Similarly, the Twelve Step myth is based upon the idea that awareness of the problem is the first step to change: For alcoholics to recognize that they are powerless evidences that an expansion of consciousness has taken place—what was previously unconscious (as a shadow complex defined by a delusion of control) becomes conscious, and they concede to their innermost self that they are alcoholic.

In the mythos of *the Alcoholic*, the insoluble dilemma of alcoholism is what leads to *an improved conscious contact with the Unconscious.* By the same token, the Fall of Adam and Eve is sometimes called *felix culpa*, a Latin phrase translated as "happy guilt," "lucky fault," or "fortunate fall." After all, the Fall made it possible for God's divine plan to unfold. Similarly, the compulsive behavior of the Anonymous Alcoholic sets in motion circumstances that lead directly to the collapse of the ego and the subsequent spiritual awakening. In both myths, the differentiation of consciousness grows out of an increasing tension of psychological opposites, leading to the fulfillment of God's "decision to become man,"[10] i.e., Self-realization.

To illustrate how the "tremendous polarity" plays out for an alcoholic, we can use a common example from AA meetings that breaks down their drinking career into three easily understandable stages: "First there is the 'fun stage.' Next is 'fun with problems,' where the fun outweighs the consequences for drinking. Finally, it is 'just problems,' when

---

[10] Jung, *CW*, vol. 11, para. 640.

the fun is all but gone and the consequences for drinking have become extremely dark and dangerous, yet they continue to drink *against their will.*"

The mythos of the Anonymous Alcoholic illustrates the increasing intensity of an insoluble psychological dilemma— mirroring what takes place in Eden. The paradisiacal state before Adam and Eve partake of the forbidden fruit parallels the time during the drinking career of alcoholics when alcohol "still works"—it's called the "fun" stage, but what they really mean is that intoxication sufficiently quenches their intangible spiritual thirst. Strange as it sounds, as alcoholics, the act of imbibing alcohol provides them with a spiritual experience not unlike the one Adam and Eve had while innocently wandering the garden, partaking freely of the fruit of the tree of life and "playing God." In the early stages of alcoholism, alcohol is a magic elixir that immediately transports the alcoholic into a mystical realm, much as we saw with Jaime as he began to explore the myth of the Ajumawi, which fostered within him a very real sense of connection he was unable to find anywhere else. In fact, drinking alcohol adds so much color to the life of alcoholics that the thought of quitting would never occur to them at this point, for it still has the power to change their perception of the world—allowing them to return to the paradisiacal state of the Garden, psychologically speaking. Thus, rather than viewing "drinking" as problematic, alcoholics unconsciously rely upon it as a solution to all of their other problems. If the newcomer expects to stay clean and sober, then the program of the Twelve Steps has to replicate what intoxication "did *for* them" in the early days, bringing about a fundamental change in their perspective on life. If they can't find a sufficient spiritual substitute, then they are destined to keep chasing "the good old days" as they try to "recapture the moments of the past."[11] Even some of the old-timers will admit that "if alcohol still worked, they'd still be using it."

For alcoholics, in the early days of drinking, the seed of conflict lies dormant—the snake hasn't come whispering—yet. Like Adam and Eve before they partook of the forbidden fruit, they are still unaware of their nakedness (sometimes quite literally), oblivious to the fact that they are in full identification with the Father/Self (unconsciously identified with the archetype of *the Alcoholic*). Since they already have an abnormal relationship with alcohol, the inherent conflict surrounding their use of it will inevitably play out over time, just like the conflict that was destined to unfold in the Garden. The magical escape that alcohol provided in the early days is so powerful that alcoholics will chase after it for many years to come despite what alcohol increasingly "does *to* them" as time passes. Sadly, the "release from care, boredom, and worry" that alcohol once provided becomes ever more elusive.[12]

Eventually, vague awareness of a dilemma creeps into the "alcoholic mind,"[13] planted there by the Self, ushering in the "fun with problems" stage. Conflict begins to emerge, but they are unclear about its root cause. Mounting consequences provide plenty of evidence to those around them that they have a drinking problem, but they still can't see it—perhaps there is an arrest, the loss of a job, or a failed marriage. Unable

---

[11] *Alcoholics Anonymous*, 151.
[12] *Alcoholics Anonymous*, 152.
[13] *Alcoholics Anonymous*, 41.

to relate anything "bad" to their drinking, denial sets in as they continue to blame others for their problems, the way Adam and Eve did when confronted by the Father. They are still unaware that alcohol has become their "solution," even though it is starting to look and feel more like the makeshift aprons of branches and leaves that Adam and Eve used "to cover their nakedness" than the quick ticket to a mystical experience that it once was. Alcoholics in this phase are in a lot of trouble, but it seems only the sober members of AA know just how dangerous and deadly the game is that has them trapped, for even as dim awareness of the conflict begins to emerge, they may still be years or even decades from realizing that it is in fact an insoluble dilemma linked directly to the psychospiritual disease of alcoholism.

As time marches on, the conflict deepens. Increasingly things get out of hand when they drink, and at some point, they'll start to experiment with ways to control it; they'll long to "drink like a [lady or a] gentleman"[14] once again, and they might even try to quit for good. Unfortunately, however, they won't be able to stop without a spiritual experience, no matter how badly they want to. Already powerless, they repeatedly tell themselves and others that "this time will be different," unable to recognize that alcohol now represents a power greater than themselves, and that they are suffering from an insoluble psychological conflict defined by a delusion of control. This ever-worsening situation finally ushers in the "just problems" phase of chronic alcoholism. Although they have been powerless over alcohol for a very long time,

---

[14] *Alcoholics Anonymous*, 31.

they now start to comprehend how grave the diagnosis is. Every night they promise themselves that "tomorrow will be different," yet with each new day they drink anyway, wearing out the "hundred alibis" that suited them just fine in earlier times.[15] They try everything they can think of to stop— religion, psychiatry, detox, rehab—they might start visiting AA meetings, but even that doesn't seem to work. Hopelessly defeated, they "pick up" even after extended periods of forced abstinence from their repeated trips to jails, hospitals, or institutions: They "always drink again, no matter what,"[16] and this fact alone makes them wonder if they haven't lost their minds. But the worst part of all is that the spiritual solution that alcohol once provided has vanished; the best they can hope for now is oblivion—"blotting out the consciousness of [their] intolerable situation as best [they can]" day after day, month after month, year after year.[17] Thus, alcoholism manifests as an impossible, deadly dilemma, mirrored in the Eden myth as Adam and Eve are forced out of the Garden and made to wander the world of sorrow, with full knowledge of their impending death.

The At-one-ment

If the myth of the Fall symbolizes the birth of the ego and the awareness of inescapable opposites, then the ego's subsequent death and rebirth into a new world of perception—the "entire psychic change" as it was called by Dr. Silkworth—is reflected

---

[15] *Alcoholics Anonymous*, 23.
[16] See *Alcoholics Anonymous*, 40-43.
[17] *Alcoholics Anonymous*, 58.

in the story of Christ and his suffering and resurrection. Jung writes:

> Individuation is an heroic and often tragic task, the most difficult of all, it involves suffering, a passion of the ego: the ordinary, empirical man we once were is burdened with the fate of losing himself in a greater dimension and being robbed of his fancied freedom of will. He suffers, so to speak, from the violence done to him by the self. ...Through the Christ-symbol, man can get to know the real meaning of his suffering: he is on the way towards realizing his wholeness. ... The drama of the archetypal life of Christ describes in symbolic images the events in the conscious life—as well as in the life that transcends consciousness—of a man who has been transformed by his higher destiny.[18]

The mythological character of Jesus, like that of the Anonymous Alcoholic, represents the ego's coming to know that the Self is running the show and learning to trust this force rather than strive against it. Like Adam and Eve and Jesus, the alcoholic ego must accept its fate of dying a spiritual death in order to gain eternal life. The Atonement of Christ paints a clear picture of "the violence done by the self" as it "robs the ego of its fancied freedom of will." Similarly, the drinking career of an alcoholic brought about "self-imposed crises that

---

[18] Jung, *CW*, vol. 11, para. 233.

[they] could neither postpone nor evade,"[19] stripping them of their delusion of control and coercing them "to turn their will and their life over to the care of God," the symbol of the Self. In fact, Jesus's prayer in Gethsemane epitomizes an ego that has "been surrendered" to the will of the higher Self: "And he went a little further, and fell on his face, and prayed, saying, O my Father, if it be possible, let this cup pass from me: nevertheless not as I will, but as thou wilt."[20] One might say that Jesus's prayer in Gethsemane is a reflection of Step Three, which includes a similar plea to one's Higher Power— always with "one more attempt, and one more failure,"[21] the ego finally capitulates, but not a moment before every other conceivable solution has been tried and found lacking.

The "violence done by the self" is what eventually collapses the ego that was birthed in Eden. It is the holiest sacrifice of all, for it makes a fusion of the psychological opposites possible, bringing to pass the at-one-ment of our perception of what has been "good" and what has been "evil" in our lives. Where the Garden of Eden myth introduced consciousness by way of a problem of opposites, the myth of the Atonement illustrates the process whereby our preconceived notions about them are cut away. Spiritual death is always a violent ordeal for the ego. Like Christ and the animal slain at Eden's gate, when the gods use the flaming sword upon us, the part of us burdened by so many judgments and opinions dies while the part of us already connected to the realm of the immortal is enlivened.

---

[19] Alcoholics Anonymous, 53.
[20] Matthew 26:39, KJV.
[21] See *Alcoholics Anonymous*, 63, 151.

16

The Mystery of Compulsion

Read psychologically, myths like the Fall and the Atonement depict how the Self disrupts the ego's intentions, frustrating its need for security and comfort. In order to wake the ego from its delusion of control, the Self must snatch away our "fancied freedom of will." In 1961, when asked to define his notion of deity, Jung responded by describing this very function of the Self: "To this day God is the name by which I designate all things which cross my willful path violently and recklessly, all things which upset my subjective views, plans and intentions, and change the course of my life for better or worse."[1] Here, Jung intentionally conflates his concept of the Self with that of the God-image, referring to the aspect of the Unconscious that alters the course the ego intends, or as Wilson wrote, renders "our little plans and designs" useless, smashing "the delusion that [we] can wrest satisfaction and happiness out of this world if [we] only manage well."[2]

It follows that the Self is most apparent when things aren't going according to plan, when our lives feel unmanageable and out of control. Jung drives home the incendiary nature of the Self's action upon the ego in his

---

[1] Cited in Herrmann, *Doorways to the Self*, 54.
[2] *Alcoholics Anonymous*, 61.

statement: "Compulsion is the great mystery of human life. It is the thwarting of our conscious will and of our reason by an inflammable element within us, appearing now as a consuming fire and now as life-giving warmth."[3] And while we always thought that whatever upsets our subjective views, plans, and intentions grows from circumstances *outside* ourselves, prompting us to petition our Higher Power for help in solving such problems, in reality the trouble emerges from *within*, arising out of the Self. Encompassing the collective unconscious, the Self also governs what happens to us individually, ensuring that everything we need to be restored to wholeness is presented—every defining conflict springs from such a place.[4] As we've seen, failing to pay attention to such nudges often results in neurosis, another of the Self's potent tools for bringing about Self-realization, or its expression into the world of form.

Edinger, too, wrote of the Self as the "supreme psychic authority" that "subordinates the ego to it," confirming that the Self is "identical with the God-image."[5] We might view our relationship to this inner deity the same way Jesus understood his relationship to the Father: "The wind blows wherever it pleases. You hear its sound, but you cannot tell where it comes from or where it is going. So it is with everyone born of

---

[3] Jung, *CW*, vol. 14, para. 151.

[4] "By far the greatest number of spontaneous synchronistic phenomena that I have had occasion to observe and analyze can easily be shown to have a direct connection with an archetype. This, in itself, is an irrepresentable, psychoid factor of the collective unconscious." (Jung, *CW*, vol. 8, para. 912). The "psychoid" was Jung's term to describe the energy that emanates throughout the cosmos, beyond the collective unconscious.

[5] Edinger, *Ego and Archetype*, 3.

[Spiritus, the breath of life]."[6] The ego relates to the Self the same way; you can feel the wind brushing your skin; you can hear it rustling the leaves and see it course along the water, but you can't see, hear, or touch the wind itself. Similarly, the ego may sense the presence of the Self; it might even make an educated guess about its function, origin, and purpose, yet it will never fully conceptualize the unconscious Self since it cannot see, touch, or hear it directly.[7]

Due to the fact that the Self is all but impossible to conceptualize, we must rely on myth, which emerges out of same unconscious place, to elucidate the meaning and purpose of our compulsions—the very thing that leads us toward improved conscious contact with the Universal Mind. The unmanageability of our lives is meant to clue the ego in to those spiritual forces that are otherwise imperceptible: Compulsion is "the great mystery of human life" because of the simple fact that it's so hard to see, even for one completely ensnared by it like a chronic alcoholic. Thus, the modern mythos of *the Alcoholic* lays open the mystery of compulsion, for the same phenomenon that tricks alcoholics into becoming powerless over alcohol is behind all of their unconscious drives, many of which persist long after the drinking problem has been resolved. In fact, every compulsive behavior, no matter how inconsequential (or downright evil) it might appear, can serve to awaken the ego from its delusion of control. *Compulsion is the doorway that opens directly into the unconscious, and to become aware of any of the compulsions that drive us is to arguably make the greatest leap in consciousness that we can*

---

[6] John 3:8.
[7] See Jung, *CW*, vol. 9ii, para. 76.

make, alcoholic or not. To admit that our lives have become unmanageable, as suggested in the first step, is to take our first foray into the objective psyche, to begin to comprehend the Great Reality about ourselves and the world around us.

The Myth of Compulsion

Thus, we could say that alcoholics and drug addicts have a spiritual advantage, for their compulsion to imbibe is heightened to the point that life becomes utterly unmanageable: They can only masquerade as "being in control" for so long; eventually it all "catches up to them," thoroughly convincing them that what they suffer from is at base a delusion of control. Trapping them in a live-or-die dilemma, King Alcohol either murders drunks in their unconscious slumber or shakes them out of it while trying. Jung provides a similar harrowing image of the mystery of compulsion, comparing the Self to a ship's captain who intentionally steers the vessel directly into dangerous seas, regardless of the ego's yearning for safety and comfort:

> There is a diabolical element which is a part of every psyche, which is the fiery center in us from which the creative or destructive influences come. ... The experience [of the] highest and lowest both come from the depths of the soul, and either bring the frail vessel of consciousness to shipwreck or carry it safely to port, with little or no assistance from us. The experience of this "center" is therefore a numinous one in its own right.[8]

---

[8] Jung, CW, vol. 9ii, paras. 135, 137.

Whenever we engage in thoughts or behaviors that we don't really choose, the Self is at the helm, steering our course from unfathomable depths. Drawing once again from the analogy that Jesus gave of *Spiritus*, compulsion is the invisible force of the Self that is apprehensible, driving the ego the way wind drives a sail, often sending us right into the eye of the storm—where real damage is done. Having been specifically formulated around many of the most common compulsive behaviors of the human race, the Twelve Steps help individuals to understand them through a spiritual lens, revealing that we only overcome our unconscious urges by increasing our awareness of them. The powerlessness and unmanageability at the base of our experience of Step One leads the ego directly into a spiritual dilemma that can only be solved by relying on the power of Step Two. An apt motto in AA reminds us that "a head full of AA and a belly full of booze don't mix"—it'll drive any real alcoholic to the gates of insanity and death. The myth of compulsions, the Twelve Steps has served to establish how vitally necessary the recognition of one's own powerlessness and unmanageability is in getting a handle on one's compulsivity. And yet, once we realize that our compulsion stems from the same energy source we petition to mollify it—the objective psyche—a whole new psychospiritual landscape opens before us: Reframing our compulsions with spiritual meaning and value, the creative influence of the Self begins to manifest, leading to the discovery of our spiritual *vocation*.

Steps One through Three address the compulsive dynamic that exists between the Self and the ego, but Steps Six and Seven provide even more compelling context of its profound mystery. Having "searched out the flaws in our makeup which caused our failure,"[9] thereby uncovering our most glaring defects through Steps Four and Five, it is suggested that we contemplate what we've accomplished up to this point. Then, becoming willing, we humbly ask God to remove our defects of character, specifically, to take "all of us, good and bad," in Steps Six and Seven.[10] And while it's true that our more subtle compulsions won't come to light right away, as recovering alcoholics and addicts we will eventually see that our powerlessness over them is bound to manifest in unmanageability nonetheless. Thus, the journey in later recovery is to learn to surrender all of our unconscious tendencies over to the care of the same paradoxical power that relieved us from our great obsession early on.

Some of us need "outside help" in order to deal with those issues that repeatedly trigger unconscious reactions in us, especially within our most intimate relationships. Such compulsions are far more common than alcoholism and addiction—*everyone* has them—but they are less discernible too, usually requiring a skilled professional to flush out and process. Jung said that "the serious problems in life … are never fully solved"; [11] our unconscious reactions are sure to provide spiritual fuel for as long as we live. And while the compulsions we uncover later on in recovery might feel less dangerous and therefore less pressing than those that drove us into "the rooms," any delusion of control that creeps up surrounding them could prove to be just as deadly—it doesn't take much for the "life giving warmth" of the numinosum to reignite into an "all-consuming flame."

---

[9] *Alcoholics Anonymous*, 64.
[10] See *Alcoholics Anonymous,* 59, 75-76.
[11] Jung, *CW*, vol. 8, para. 771.

Vocation, The Creative Influence

The last few chapters have delineated the dark, destructive side of the Self as it pushes the ego toward transformation, but we mustn't overlook the fact that it is a creative, life-giving element that underlies the Self's insidious ploy. Like the lucky ones who see the value of working regularly with a skilled therapist or engaging in the analytical process, only those who are driven to it actually take all 12 of the Steps, usually doing so "with the desperation of drowning men"[12] because they are aware, on a very deep level, just how thin the line is that separates serenity from insanity. In such cases, the Self has demanded that they become "more conscious" by shattering their ego's grip on reality, decimating their sense of safety and comfort and literally forcing them into a new way of life: Wilson says that we arrived at a place where "there was *nothing left* but to pick up the simple kit of tools laid at our feet."[13]

The reason the Self pushes us so is because, seeing reliance upon a higher power a fool's errand, the inflated ego must be thoroughly convinced of its need for spiritual help. Wilson describes alcoholics' greatest obstacle as being their preconceived notions surrounding spirituality:

> Besides a seeming inability to accept much on faith, we often found ourselves handicapped by obstinacy, sensitiveness, and unreasoning prejudice. Many of us have been so touchy that even casual reference to spiritual things

[12] *Alcoholics Anonymous*, 28. Jung's said that "only the 'complete' person knows how unbearable man is to himself." Jung, *CW*, vol. 9ii, para. 125.
[13] *Alcoholics Anonymous*, 25. Italics mine.

made us bristle with antagonism. This sort of thinking had to be abandoned. Though some of us resisted, we found no great difficulty in casting aside such feelings. Faced with alcoholic destruction, we soon became as open minded on spiritual matters as we had tried to be on other questions. In this respect alcohol was a great persuader. It finally beat us into a state of reasonableness. Sometimes this was a tedious process; we hope no one else will be prejudiced for as long as some of us were.[14]

Once repelled by even casual references to the things of the Spirit, recovered alcoholics are engendered with an almost monkish discipline. Having discovered their vocation, they are able to dedicate their lives to a spiritual program with the same fervor that they used to have "drinking and using," displaying an astonishing commitment to their new way of life. Yet, as long as one remains dedicated to spirits, they generally find the idea of living by spiritual principles repulsive. On a psychological level, it is the Self, demanding proper relationship to it, that drives the alcoholic ego to the brink of disaster so as to dismantle this prejudice. A stark fact most alcoholics and addicts must face is that years of anguish might have been avoided if they had been more open-minded toward religious ideas. And yet, anyone who has tapped into the creative influence of the numinosum will readily admit that the only way they could discard their old way of thinking and being was by the painstaking work of ego collapse at depth, a

---

[14] *Alcoholics Anonymous*, 47-48.

tedious process that only the Self has patience, wisdom, and mercy to carry out.

For alcoholics in particular, the Self does the beating— the *ism* is just the hammer. At once life-affirming and deadly, with each devastating blow the groundwork is laid for a "wonderfully effective spiritual structure [to be] built."[15] Even though the ego puts up a good fight, Jung tells us that in the end the Self always wins:

> The Self, in its efforts at Self-realization, reaches out beyond the ego-personality on all sides; because of its all-encompassing nature it is brighter and darker than the ego, and accordingly confronts us with problems which we would like to avoid. Either one's moral courage fails, or one's insight, or both, until in the end fate decides. The ego never lacks moral and rational counterarguments, which one cannot and should not set aside so long as it is possible to hold on to them. For you only feel yourself on the right road ... when you have become the victim of a decision made over your head or in defiance of the heart. From this we can see the numinous power of the Self, which can hardly be experienced in any other way. For this reason the experience of the Self is always a defeat for the ego.[16]

---

[15] *Alcoholics Anonymous*, 47.
[16] Jung, *CW*, vol. 14, para. 778.

Our defining problems are uniquely tailored to us, emerging from the unconscious Self. Shrouded by our judgments about our character, our moral convictions, and our inability to live up to the standard that we've set for ourselves or for others, such insoluble conflicts are meant to be unbearably painful, and yet a desire to escape the pain is never enough to solve them. For even after the ego realizes its need to be recreated, it still must accept the fact that of itself, it lacks the power to do so. Just as the conflict stirred up by the Self that leads to alcoholism or addiction may make the ego willing, the power to change must also come from that incendiary element within the psyche—the same power that is so evident when we are at our worst, when we are being led like a lamb to the slaughter, is what ignites a fundamental change in our attitude and perspective.[17] Thus, Jung encourages us to hold out for as long as we can, for we can never get placed on the path until we become "fully convinced that a decision has been made over our head and in defiance of our heart"—the essence of Step One. Compulsion is the only thing powerful enough to defeat the ego, and one is unlikely to experience the numinosum any other way.

---

[17] See Jung, *CW*, vol. 14, par. 778. *Alcoholics Anonymous*, 60.

17

Doorways to the Self

As we saw in the last chapter, to be driven is to be under the influence of the numinosum. And while compulsion is among the most potent tools that the Self uses to grab the ego's attention, ironically, compulsions develop when the ego makes its own unconscious attempts to cope with the Self's impossible demands. Whenever a compulsion crops up, life becomes unmanageable, causing one to lose control over the mind, the body, and the emotions—a perilous state especially for recovering alcoholics and addicts. Such lapses in conscious awareness are what Wilson called "bouts of self," the core spiritual dilemma that all humans face:

> Selfishness—self-centeredness! That, we think, is the root of our troubles. Driven by a hundred forms of fear, self-delusion, self-seeking, and self-pity, we step on the toes of our fellows and they retaliate. Sometimes they hurt us, seemingly without provocation, but we invariably find that at some time in the past we have made decisions based on self which later placed us in a position to be hurt.

> So our troubles, we think, are basically
> of our own making. They arise out of ourselves,
> and the alcoholic is an extreme example of self-
> will run riot, though he usually doesn't think
> so.[1]

As a manifestation of the shadow, selfishness sits at the heart of our unconscious compulsions, and like many attributes of the inflated ego, alcoholics and addicts are guilty of taking it to the extreme. And yet, selfishness is not something we can simply set aside because we've decided to walk a spiritual path: Traits we hold that hinder our progress are usually survival mechanisms that stem from instinct, selfishness included; the conflict of duty that develops around them is what leads to an expansion of consciousness. Edward Edinger, who was a biologist long before he became a Jungian analyst, reminds us that "all the facts of biology and psychology teach us that every individual unit of life is self-centered to the core."[2] And while our selfishness can be damaging to our relationships and painful to acknowledge, purging ourselves of it is not feasible, as anyone who has tried can attest.

Wilson held selfishness to be particularly troublesome for alcoholics, explaining that to engage in selfish behaviors poses the greatest threat to one's sobriety, making it a deadly proposition: "Above everything, we alcoholics must be rid of this selfishness. We must, or it kills us." But Bill was self-aware enough to recognize that there is "no way of entirely getting

---

[1] *Alcoholics Anonymous,* 62.
[2] Edinger, *Ego and Archetype,* 161.

rid of self without [God's] aid." Cognizant of the insoluble nature of what he clearly depicts as a psychological dilemma as problematic as alcoholism itself, Wilson admits: "Many of us had moral and philosophical convictions galore, but we could not live up to them even though we would have liked to. Neither could we reduce our self-centeredness much by wishing or trying on our own power. We had to have God's help."[3] Wilson sensed that the solution to our unconscious compulsions, including self-centeredness, is not didactic at all—no amount of spiritual discipline will make one less selfish by nature.

A Portal into the Universal Mind

As it turns out, the Jungians have wrestled with the same quandary, offering helpful insight on how to deal with our selfishness. Edinger explains that to become aware of one's selfishness is the essence of our *myth of expanding consciousness*: "What is required is not the extirpation of selfishness, which is impossible, but rather that it become wedded to consciousness."[4] Realizing the extent of one's selfishness, one brings a small piece of the unconscious Self into the light, and taking into account the effects of such behavior on others, one becomes less self-centered, even if only momentarily. Steven Herrmann also ruminates on the insolubility of our unconscious drives in his book *Doorways to the Self*. Borrowing from the text of William James' *Varieties*,

---

[3] *Alcoholics Anonymous*, 62.
[4] Edinger, *Ego and Archetype*, 161.

Dr. Herrmann describes how shadow traits like selfishness are in fact the gateway "to the deeper reaches [that] the founders of all the world's great religions pass through to arrive at their insights ... the subliminal doorway that opens up to the mother-sea of all truly objective thoughts."[5] The root cause of all of our shortcomings—including one's powerlessness over alcohol and the resultant unmanageability—selfishness represents our most direct portal into the unconscious, the key to unlocking improved conscious contact with the Universal Mind inasmuch as it is the attribute of the shadow that is perhaps the easiest to spot.

Thus, Jung would write that our foray into the unconscious begins when we take an honest look at our own selfish and self-centered behavior:

> The integration or humanization of the Self is initiated from the conscious side by our making ourselves aware of our selfish aims; we examine our motives and try to form as complete and objective a picture as possible of our own nature. It is an act of self-recollection, a gathering together of what is scattered, of all the things in us that have never been properly related, and a coming to terms with oneself with a view to achieving full consciousness... Self-recollection, however, is about the hardest and most repellant thing there is for man, who

---

[5] Herrmann, *Doorways*, 249. Jung said that "The first step on the way to individuation consists in the discrimination between [oneself] and the shadow." Jung, *CW*, vol. 9ii, para. 19.

is predominantly unconscious. Human nature
has an invincible dread of becoming more
conscious of itself. What nevertheless drives
us to it is the self, which demands sacrifice by
sacrificing itself to us.[6]

The humanization of the Self (i.e., Self-realization) involves the
ego's integration of aspects of the unconscious, initiated from
the *unconscious* side whenever the Self leads the ego into
any number of compulsive, self-serving behaviors. Then, from
the *conscious* side, the ego responds by reflecting upon those
very behaviors that make life unmanageable, behaviors that
are always rooted in selfishness. The humanization of the Self
takes place as the ego realizes that it has been compelled by a
supraordinate psychic complex to engage in such behaviors in
the first place, thus wedding them to consciousness.

Having described the selfish and self-centered
alcoholic, Wilson presents his method for coming to terms
with selfishness, an approach similar to the introspective
attitude Jung recommends: In Steps Four and Five, we "get
down to causes and conditions [by making an extensive]
personal inventory."[7] Contrary to popular opinion, however,
we don't examine our selfish aims, either with a sponsor or
a therapist, so that we can "work on them," or try to "make
ourselves better" by eradicating selfishness—the mystery
of compulsion will render us powerless to do so anyway.

[6] Jung, *CW*, vol. 11, para. 400.
[7] *Alcoholics Anonymous*, 76. In the Big Book, Wilson's great treatise on
selfishness directly precedes his instructions on how to work Step Four.
See *Alcoholics Anonymous*, 60-63.

Because we are "driven to act and free to reflect," the true path to enlightenment will beckon us to reflect upon our selfish behavior while at the same time holding enough space for the recognition that the ego is powerless to change it.

Still, wedding our selfishness to consciousness feels so abhorrent, none but the most desperate cases become willing, even within the fellowships. The inventory Wilson suggested in Steps Four and Five guides us "to examine our motives and try to form as complete and objective a picture as possible of our own nature." Having done our level best to formulate such a perspective, Steps Six, Seven, Eight, and Nine represent the only viable actions the ego can take to combat what compels it—becoming willing; first, we ask God to "remove from [us] every single defect of character which stands in the way of [our] usefulness to [God] and [our] fellows,"[8] after which we set out to make a full and complete amends "wherever possible." After that, we'll find ourselves well positioned to fulfill our "real purpose [which is] to be of maximum service to God and our fellows," carrying the message, as suggested in Step Twelve. As formulaic as such a course of action might make spiritual transformation sound, it is the most difficult thing we will ever do—"the hardest and most repellent thing there is for us humans," says Jung, who are "predominantly unconscious." Wilson would agree: "It is simple, but not easy; a price had to be paid. It meant the destruction of self-centeredness. [We] must turn in all things to the Father of Light who presides over us all."[9]

---

[8] *Alcoholics Anonymous*, 76.
[9] *Alcoholics Anonymous*, 14.

Emulating the Self

The Self is the central axis in the psyche, driving the ego according to the dictates of its own wishes, often to the ego's detriment. In this way, the Self can be thought of as being ultimately "selfish," i.e., "absorbed in fulfilling its own wishes." Jung highlights this curious phenomenon, explaining how the ego-centrism that is so evident in the life of alcoholics is in fact an echo of the "Self-centrism" of the Universal Mind: "The unconscious is undoubtedly older and more original than consciousness, and for this reason one could just as well call the egocentrism of consciousness a reflection or imitation of the 'self'-centrism of the unconscious."[10] The "selfishness" of the Unconscious is made obvious by the fact that it is willing to sacrifice the ego, risking insanity and/or death in order to achieve its goal of Self-realization.

The adventure of the Anonymous Alcoholic provides helpful context regarding this so-called "Self-centrism": The selfish alcoholic, driven by an overarching mental obsession and physical craving for alcohol, is a reflection of the Universal Mind's yearning for expression through the ego, its thirst to manifest itself into consciousness. According to Edinger, since the ego copies the "centrism" of the Self, it is bound to become more conscious of that which it emulates: "If egocentrism is the ego's imitation of the Self, then it will be by conscious acceptance of this tendency that the ego will become aware of that which it is imitating; namely, the transpersonal center

---

[10] Jung, *CW*, vol. 14, para. 660. *Ego-centrism* is the false belief that the ego is the central, most powerful complex in the psyche, when in reality, it is the Self who holds that position.

and unity of individuality, the Self."[11] Paradoxically, the more selfish one is, the more likely one is to become aware of one's unconscious drives, and the better chance one has of attaining Self-realization or enlightenment. Thus, selfishness is not just the root of our troubles, it is also the seat of spiritual vitality.

Edinger describes how in practice, examining ourselves from the point of view of the objective psyche allows us to cultivate a "higher form" of selfishness:

> The majority of patients in psychotherapy need to learn how to be more effectively selfish and more effective in the use of their own personal power; they need to accept responsibility for the fact of being centers of power and effectiveness. So-called selfish or egocentric behavior which expresses itself in demands made on others is not effective conscious self-centeredness or conscious individuality. We demand from others only what we fail to give ourselves. If we have insufficient self-love or self-prestige, our need expresses itself unconsciously by coercive tactics toward others. And often the coercion occurs under the guise of virtue, love, or altruism. Such unconscious selfishness is ineffectual and destructive to oneself and others. It fails to achieve its purpose because it is blind, without awareness of itself.[12]

---

[11] Edinger, *Ego and Archetype*, 160.
[12] Edinger, *Ego and Archetype*, 160-61.

Edinger's notion of *unconscious selfishness* is comparable to what is often called "self-centered fear" in Twelve Step spaces: Afraid of not having our basic emotional and psychological needs met—to be loved and respected—we make dishonest and manipulative demands upon others. Being unconsciously motivated, that sort of selfishness is ineffectual, even damaging. On the other hand, as the ego comes to recognize that it is not the central axis in the psyche, cultivating what Edinger calls "conscious effective self-centeredness," we find ourselves empowered in our service to others, embodying a message that through reliance upon a higher power, their core needs can be met, as ours have.

C

Conclusion

The Shadow of a Figure of Light

The God-image is the foundation of the human psyche, no matter the particulars of its conception for any individual in any moment in history, and the emergence of the Twelve Steps, alongside Jung's science of individuation, suggests that as a species, we are more prepared than ever to have the veil pulled back, as more and more of us conceive of "the gods as a psychic factor." Metaphorically speaking, the ego has been chipping away at the formless unconscious the way a sculptor shapes an indeterminate chunk of granite, and the closer the artist gets to revealing the form she intends, the less imagination one needs to "see it." The image of God that is slowly emerging over the course of eons is turning out to be the most beautiful self-portrait we could ever imagine.

As the ego labors to bring more of the unconscious into the light, the religious figures meant to reflect the transformation process become more differentiated as well— they point more directly to our individual experience. Thus, the mythical tale taking place today is of our own awakenings: The shrouded symbols describing transformation we've inherited from the myths of generations past are being replaced by our own unique articulation of the primordial experience itself; such is the nature of each of our *myths of expanding consciousness.*[1] In our efforts to express the ineffable, we experience it more profoundly; sharing our stories, we gain a deeper understanding and appreciation of the miracle that is taking place in this very moment. As we've seen, every personal adventure to discover an authentic connection to the numinosum, the same power that has always given myth its place in the world, is a journey of psychological development. After all, "psychology and religion are complementary paths to the same goal—Self-realization of the unconscious," as Dr. Herrmann points out in *Doorways to the Self.* [2]

Projections of the Self

Hence, we can expect the God-image to continue to morph in the collective imagination so long as human consciousness continues to expand and we continue to tell the tale of *what we used to be like, what happened, and what we're like now.* Jung helped to usher in this new approach to the God-concept when he superimposed the Self, a conception he borrowed from a multitude of influences spanning the globe and history of the world, with his own notion of spirituality. However, Jung tells us that he wasn't the only person in the modern West to

---

[1] Jung confirms that as the religious process becomes more differentiated, the myth can be "relieved of [its] principle encumbrances." See Jung, *Letters*, vol. 2, p. 484.

[2] Herrmann, *Doorways*, 203.

Conclusion

depict the emergence of the Self; it had already began bubbling up through the writings of other modern authors who hinted at its presence through characters in their fictional narratives, opening his mind further to the individualized nature of the emerging God-image. However, those authors' portraits of the Self had come about unconsciously, as we saw in the case of Nietzsche, whose relationship to his own shadow we touched upon in chapter 11. Jung explains in *Psychological Types* that

> in unconscious fantasies the self often appears as a supraordinate or ideal personality, having somewhat the relationship of Faust to Goethe or Zarathustra to Nietzsche. For the sake of idealization the archaic features of the self are represented as being separate from the "higher" self, as for instance Mephistopheles in Goethe, Epimetheus in Spitteler, and in Christian psychology the devil or Antichrist. In Nietzsche, Zarathustra discovered his shadow in the "Ugliest Man."[3]

While the notion of "the divine Self" has been contemplated in the East for millennia, Jung encountered an image of Self that could bridge the gap between the most ancient conceptions of God (what he called *the primitive*) with that of the modern West, one that fused the dark, primordial powers of the unconscious with those of the light of modern human intellect. Here again, we see how our culture's religious myths provide

[3] Jung, *CW,* vol. 6, para. 706.

245

a stark reflection of our individual psychology, for whenever an author, a psychologist, or a prophet splits the God-image into a higher and lower aspect, either within a narrative or through a paradoxical image, it is an unconscious portrayal of the Self. Psychologically speaking, the shadowy half of the image that is cut off is illustrative of our inability to understand our own unconscious compulsivity; in an attempt to *idealize our own higher self*, we deny having any real connection to the dark and archaic urges that make up so much of the human psyche and that is reflected in the characters of our stories. In Nietzsche's *Thus Spoke Zarathustra*, for instance, the Ugliest Man "murdered God" for having shown compassion in the face of depravity. We see the same tendency in our religious myths as well. For example, the God of the Old Testament named "Yahweh," the unyielding Creature who punished Job (and later Jesus), cuts off his *Luciferian opponent*, who is then ironically banished to outer darkness for encompassing many of the same amoral traits as the not-so-benevolent God-figure.[4] And just as we tend to deny the existence of our individual shadow, rather than seeking to reconcile the antithetical, paradoxical energy expressed through these mythical images, the shadow of the figure of light is cut off, mirroring our refusal to accept our own innate darkness.

We see a similar propensity in the mythos of the Twelve Steps, for the fractured God-image typical of the West is the same one that Wilson couldn't stomach and the same one

---

[4] Recall Jung said, "the Christ-symbol lacks wholeness in the modern psychological sense since it does not include the dark side of things but specifically excludes it in the form of a Luciferian opponent." Jung, *CW*, vol. 9ii, par. 74.

the vast majority bring into our first Twelve Step meeting. Faced with the impossible task of relying upon "this particular conception"[5] to rescue us, whom we can't fully trust, we split the image by "swinging violently" toward its higher aspect and, like the Church fathers did many centuries ago, ignore what we imagine to be its dark and destructive side.[6] We see something of Wilson's own misgivings regarding the paradoxical nature of the God-image poking through in the wording he chose for Step Three: "We made a decision to turn our will and our lives over to *the care of God* as we understood him." Perhaps without realizing it, Wilson turns away from what he perceived as the morally unreliable aspect of his Higher Power and instead focuses on its love and concern—distrusting of the dark, compulsive nature of his own psyche, Wilson makes an unconscious attempt to idealize God's, and thus his own higher self.

And yet, we've seen that a God-image that lacks wholeness is like a broken electrical circuit, for it also lacks numinosity. The same goes for us: Whenever we refuse to accept both sides of the Great Reality, we are bound to feel restless, irritable, discontented. Thus, unbeknownst to us, in the beginning of our journey into recovery, it was the archetype of *the Alcoholic,* birthed out of the Universal Mind into Wilson's myth, who came to the rescue, for it is an image which bridges the chasm between the light and dark aspects of our own psyche, reflecting the paradox of how a psychic complex, a human being, and an image of God can be both light and dark, good and evil, at the same time.

---

[5] *Alcoholics Anonymous*, 45.
[6] See Jung, *CW*, vol. 9ii, paras. 77-78.

Making the Darkness Conscious

Our rejection of *the Czar of Heaven* is a psychological reaction not unlike Nietzsche's—rejecting the unpredictable aspect of the deity in favor of something more palatable is in essence killing off the God-image—something all of us are guilty of inasmuch as the *Czar of Heaven* is a reflection of our relationship to our own darkness. And yet, it is the psychological nature of Wilson's myth that opened up a path for him that led to wholeness, for as we've seen, he would go on to present the *archaic features of the Self* as a supraordinate psychological entity, characterizing *the primitive* as "the sort of thinking" that dominates "the alcoholic mind," which "can only be described as plain insanity."[7] So while he splits the God-image in "Bill's Story," the fact that he circles back to its archaic form later, through the shadow of the Anonymous Alcoholic, allowed him to retain an essential balance of the highest and the lowest of human nature in his myth, and thus to tap into the transformative power of the numinosum.

We see masterfully illustrated throughout Wilson's text how religious symbols mirror psychic states, and he guides his readers toward the discovery of the Self as it manifests in our lives through the unconscious tendencies that drive us on both sides of the psychospiritual spectrum. To see how Wilson's characterization of *the archaic* in the Big Book reveals the presence of the paradoxical Self requires an exploration of his myth from the same psychological perspective that Jung employed. Assuming Wilson was unaware of Jung's notion of

[7] *Alcoholics Anonymous*, 41, 48.

the Self, his projection of it shows up right where we would expect it, as the shadow of the book's archetypal protagonist— that anonymous character that Bill purposefully crafted as a psychological mirror for his alcoholic readers. Wilson had become so familiar with aspects of his own darkness that it allowed him to give clear voice to *the archaic*, personified through the various metaphorical characters we encounter in the Big Book, such as the "boy whistling in the dark," "King Alcohol," and "the hideous Four Horseman."[8]

And yet, it's easy to overlook the fact that Wilson formulated another far more numinous shadow character than even these, that highly abstracted image that he called "self"—the driving force of the alcoholic mind—unaware that in doing so he was complementing Jung's conception of that same archetypal image.[9] For, like Jung, Wilson's "self" illustrates the evil machinations of the Universal Mind to make *conscious contact* with the ego, setting the process of Self-realization in motion from the unconscious side of the veil: "When we became alcoholics, crushed by a self-imposed crisis that we could neither postpone nor evade, we had to fearlessly face the proposition that God is either everything, or else He is nothing. God either is, or He isn't. What was our choice to be?"[10] The "we" Wilson refers to is the Anonymous Alcoholic, that modern mythical character reflective of the alcoholic ego, and by employing his use of the word "self" as a reference to the same archetypal Self that Jung discovered,

---

[8] *Alcoholics Anonymous*, 151.
[9] It is possible that Wilson borrowed the term "self" from his reading of James' *Varieties*, who speaks of "the divided self."
[10] *Alcoholics Anonymous*, 53.

the "inner empirical deity," the dynamic between these two psychological entities is illustrated perfectly—the ego is forced to endure "the violence done by the Self" through a multitude of "Self-imposed crises" that it (the ego) does not create and cannot avoid. Jung explained that such crises "confront us in situations where there are insoluble conflicts. … This means, in other words, that … the ego is a suffering bystander who decides nothing but must submit to a decision and surrender unconditionally."[11] What the Wilsonian myth helps to clarify is that humans will find no relief from any of our "great obsessions" until we surrender to *the archaic* in our own psyche, conceding that it is far more powerful than our most sincere desire to behave in any certain way. In *Alcoholics Anonymous*, the primitive, instinctual aspect of "the power greater than" is what Wilson called "self," a personification of his own darkness.

Recognizing Wilson's projection of the Self allows us to go deeper in our understanding of the dark, hidden reaches of our own individual psyche and to plug into the spiritual potential stored there. On the surface, the journey of the Twelve Steps looks to be about finding a safe passage through the dilemma defined by the opposites "to drink or not to drink"—a worthy and necessary spiritual endeavor for those who find it to be an impossible dilemma. However, by providing an easy-to-read road map into *the archaic aspect of the psyche*, Wilson shows us how to wed our unconscious compulsion to consciousness, propelling one towards greater Self-realization long after the drinking problem has dissipated.

---

[11] Jung, *CW*, vol. 9ii, para. 79.

Beyond "to drink and not to drink," humankind is awash in any number of insoluble psychic conflicts that are central to the mythos of the Anonymous Alcoholic—instinct and spirit, good and evil, selfish and self-less behavior, among countless others—all providing a potential passageway into *improved conscious contact with the Unconscious Self*. The task before us, then, is to continue the search for where *the archaic* manifests in our lives and to wed it to consciousness as best we can.

A Play of Light and Dark

As close as Wilson was to the eternal fountainhead, it appears that his own conception of the God-image never made that final leap, as Jung did when he recapitulated the dichotomous facets of the primordial experience into a single, paradoxical unity he called *the Self*. Jung illustrates what such a conception looks like:

> Like all archetypes, the Self has a paradoxical, antimonial character. It is male and female, old man and child, powerful and helpless, large and small. The Self is a true "complexio oppositorum," though this does not mean that it is anything like as contradictory in itself. It is quite possible that the seeming paradox is nothing but a reflection of the enantiodromian changes of the conscious attitude which can have a favorable or an unfavorable effect on the whole. ... [The Self represents] a union of

> opposites, it can also appear as a united duality, in the form, for instance, of tao as the interplay of yang and yin, or of the hostile brothers, or of the hero and his adversary (arch-enemy, dragon). ... Empirically, therefore, the Self appears as a play of light and shadow, although conceived as a totality, a unity in which the opposites are united.[12]

Personifying the dynamic that permeates the Cosmos, the Self is a field of energy projected into a form that the human ego can relate to, epitomized by the dichotomous anthropomorphic symbols we've explored: the God-image, the Trickster, and *the Alcoholic*. The Self may appear as a paradoxical play on any commonly held pair of opposites—man/woman, old/young, light/dark, powerful/powerless, as well as *wounded healer* and *sober drunk*. The paradoxical nature of such symbols is meant to be problematic for the ego, sharpening awareness of whatever insoluble dilemma that the unconscious has used to snare it. Edinger writes that "paradox is an affront to the logic consciousness, so it's a deliberate defeat for the rational ego... Paradoxes [always] point to the Self."[13] Every spiritual tale— even our own—is composed of qualities that are impossible for us to reconcile; such paradoxes become an important instrument the Self deploys in our quest for enlightenment: "Paradox does more justice to the unknowable than clarity

---

[12] Jung, *CW*, vol. 9ii, para. 355.

[13] Edward F. Edinger and Joan Dexter Blackmer, *The Mysterium Lectures: A Journey through C.G. Jung's Mysterium Coniunctionis*, Studies in Jungian Psychology by Jungian Analysts 66 (Toronto: Inner City Books, 1995), 55.

can do," explains Jung, "for uniformity of meaning robs the mystery of its darkness and sets it up as something that is known."[14] When the Mystery is robbed of its darkness, it loses the transformative power it might have otherwise evoked.

Wilson tells us that right before he checked himself into Towns for the last time, he had taken a "plunge into the dark,"[15] the common starting point for every spiritual adventure. Jung said that to escape that bitter morass, "you have got to cling to the Good, otherwise the devil devours you."[16] The "higher Self," symbolized by the figure of light Wilson cried out to in desperation to relieve him from his ordeal, is a reflection of the supraordinate psychological entity that empowers the ego to transcend its mired state. However, "clinging to the Good" will only get us so far, especially if we suffer from an insoluble psychological dilemma like alcoholism or addiction. Those who live on a paradoxical knife-edge (drunk *and* sober) must adopt an image that "symbolizes the suitable fusion of the pairs of opposites in a way that makes it possible for us to function in a civilized society without shutting out the primitive," as Jung suggested to Jaime. Contemplating a figure of light by itself isn't enough to satisfy our insatiable craving for wholeness. Thus, the religious images we connect to ultimately must allow for the integration of certain dark, archaic, instinctive aspects of our nature as well—those most ancient parts of ourselves, of our psyche. For the higher power that we surrender to, the power greater than ourselves mentioned in Step Two, can't

---

[14] Jung, *CW*, vol. 11, para. 417.
[15] *Alcoholics Anonymous*, 8.
[16] Jung, *Letters*, vol. 2, p. 135.

THE SHADOW OF A FIGURE OF LIGHT

be *fully harnessed* until we learn to accept the Dark Power within that drove us to become power-*less* in Step One—the Self—playing an antithetical role in the divine drama we've been cast in.

As for Wilson, with his "self" and the "higher power," he contemplated a pair of images that brought the highest and lowest of his own nature into full account, fusing them within the light of altruistic service "to the still suffering alcoholic"— even though for him (as for many of us) their coupling into a paradoxical image of God probably never escaped the unconscious. And so, while Wilson splits the God-image throughout the Big Book, in the end his projection of *the archaic* into the alcoholic mind would prove to be sufficient, for it represents the dark side of Cosmogonic Energy as being equally powerful as any of our figures of light. Allowing for the emergent energies of the collective unconscious to be divinely balanced in his conception of psychological transformation, Wilson's myth spawned an image charged with enough spiritual tension to bring about psychic change for generations of mythless Westerners.

Thus, the Twelve Steps, even with its "inadequate conception" of God, has proven to be adequate enough to save millions because it is accompanied by that paradoxical image of wholeness, the archetype of *the Alcoholic,* whose transformative power we experience *consciously* for the first time when we finally utter out loud words that spark an immediate expansion of spiritual consciousness—"I am an alcoholic." As Steven Herrmann explains, "[Unconsciously] identifying with any archetype of the transpersonal psyche can be dangerous psychologically; being conscious of one's shadow is perhaps a more modest way to achieve a wider consciousness of the wholeness of the personality."[17] For alcoholics and drug addicts, modesty was never written into our DNA, but the minute we concede to our innermost selves that we are powerless, we consciously *dis*-identify with the archaic aspect of the archetype, putting a halt to the havoc it has been wreaking in our lives. In that moment, we also make a significant part of the shadow conscious, thereby lighting upon the path to Self-realization. Thus, the archetype of *the Alcoholic*, personifying the dualistic energy of the collective unconscious, evokes transformative power in our lives long before we ever come to believe that a figure of Light will do it.

The transformative power of the Self is only made apparent in the midst of the most profound paradoxes such as *the Alcoholic* embodies. Similar antimonies are woven throughout the Twelve Step myth, among them, the oft-used phrase "sober alcoholic" is probably the most apparent, closely followed by "grateful alcoholic," indicative of one's connection to the antithetical energy embodied by the archetype of *the Alcoholic*. Overall, Twelve Step experience confirms Jung's statement that "One does not become enlightened by imagining figures of light, but by making the darkness conscious."[18] And while the vast majority of us tend to idealize the higher self, leaving only our "good" side within view, we might endeavor to explore the dark side of our personality as well, to uncover for ourselves what role the shadow plays in our own quest for expanding consciousness. Evidencing how

---

[17] Herrmann, *Doorways*, 200.
[18] Jung, *CW*, vol. 13, para. 335.

powerful such an approach is are decades of the most glaring kind of selfish and self-centered behavior giving way to the plethora of authentic spiritual awakenings such as we see wholesale in the Twelve Step fellowships—answering how it comes to be that utterly selfish and self-centered people like us can get set on the path of enlightenment, notwithstanding all the damage wrought to our personal relationships and communities. Very often one hears in a meeting, "I'm glad I didn't get what I deserved"; many who are far more worthy won't ever make it "to the rooms," let alone uncover the mysteries of the Great Reality and unleash the creative powers of the Universe.

The path of enlightenment diverges from where we initially expected it to go, cutting right through the middle of the most depraved parts of our selves. In the words of the Greek philosopher Heraclitus: "It is the opposite which is good for us, the way up and the way down are the same."[19]

---

[19] Cited in Jung, *CW*, vol. 6, para. 708.

C

Bibliography

Alcoholics Anonymous, ed. *"Pass It on": The Story of Bill Wilson and How the A.A. Message Reached the World*. New York: Alcoholics Anonymous World Services, 1984.

———. "The A.A. Grapevine." *The Bill W. – Carl Jung Letters*, January 1963. https://speakingofjung.com/blog/2015/11/13/the-bill-w-carl-jung-letters.

Alcoholics Anonymous. 1st ed. New York City: Works Publishing Co., 1939.

Alcoholics Anonymous: The Story of How Many Thousands of Men and Women Have Recovered from Alcoholism. 4th ed. New York City: Alcoholics Anonymous World Services, 2001.

Angulo, Gui de. *The Old Coyote of Big Sur, The Life of Jaime de Angulo*. Richmond, CA: CA Palm, 1995.

———. *Indians in Overalls*. "Afterword" by Gui de Angulo, San Francisco: City Light Books, 1990.

———. *Jaime in Taos: The Taos Papers of Jaime de Angulo*. San Francisco: City Light Books, 1985.

Ayto, John. *Dictionary of Word Origins*. New York: Arcade Publishing, 2011.

Bair, D. *Jung: A Biography*. 1ˢᵗ Back Bay paperback ed. New York: Bay Back Books, 2004.

Bluhm, Amy Colwell, "Verification of C.G. Jung's analysis of Rowland Hazard and the history of Alcoholics Anonymous," *Journal of the American Psychological Association* 2006, Vol. 9, No. 4, 313–324.

Boyd, Robert, and Peter J. Richerson. "Transmission Coupling Mechanisms: Cultural Group Selection." *Philosophical Transactions of the Royal Society of London. Series B, Biological Sciences* 365, no. 1559 (December 12, 2010): 3787–95.

Buckskin, Floyd and Benson, Arlene. "The Contemporary Use of Psychoactive Mushrooms in Northern California," *Journal of California and Great Basin Anthropology*, 2005, vol. 25, No. 1, pp. 87-92.

C., Chuck, and Charles A. Chamberlain. *A New Pair of Glasses*. Irvine, CA: New-Look Publishing Co., 2009.

Campbell, Joseph. *The Masks of God: Oriental Mythology*, Novato, CA: New World Library, 2021.

———. *The Masks of God: Primitive Mythology*, Novato, CA: New World Library, 2021.

———. *The Masks of God: Occidental Mythology*, Novato, CA: New World Library, 2021.

———. *The Hero with a Thousand Faces*. 3rd ed. Bollingen Series XVII. Novato, CA: New World Library, 2008.

———. *The Inner Reaches of Outer Space: Metaphor as Myth and as Religion*. First paperback printing. Novato, CA: New World Library, 2012.

———. *The Masks of God. 4: Creative Mythology*. Harmondsworth, UK: Penguin, 1991.

Campbell, Joseph, Eugene C. Kennedy, and Joseph Campbell. *Thou Art That: Transforming Religious Metaphor*. The Collected Works of Joseph Campbell. Novato, CA: New World Library, 2001.

Campbell, Joseph, and David Kudler. *Pathways to Bliss: Mythology and Personal Transformation*. Novato, CA: New World Library, 2004.

Campbell, Joseph, Bill D. Moyers, and Betty S. Flowers. *The Power of Myth*. First Anchor Books Edition. New York: Anchor Books, 1991.

Capra, Fritjof. *The Tao of Physics: An Exploration of the Parallels between Modern Physics and Eastern Mysticism*. 5th ed. Boston: Shambhala, 2010.

Driberg, Tom. "The Mystery of Moral Re-Armament: A Study of Frank Buchman and His Movement." Secker & Warburg, n.d. https://en.wikipedia.org/wiki/Oxford_Group#cite_note-driberg-64-2.

Eckhart, Meister, and Houston Smith. *Meister Eckhart: The Essential Sermons, Commentaries, Treatises and Defense*. Translated by Edmund Colledge and Bernard McGinn. New edition. New York: Paulist Press, 1981.

Edinger, Edward F. *Ego and Archetype: Individuation and the Religious Function of the Psyche*. Reissue edition. Boston: Shambhala, 2017.

Edinger, Edward. From a talk called *Gnosticism and Early Christianity,* delivered by Edward Edinger at the C.G. Jung Institute in Los Angeles in 1994, reprinted with permission. The talks are available for purchase on the Jungian Institute of Los Angeles webpage.

Edinger, Edward F., and Joan Dexter Blackmer. *The Mysterium Lectures: A Journey through C.G. Jung's Mysterium Coniunctionis*. Studies in Jungian Psychology by Jungian Analysts 66. Toronto: Inner City Books, 1995.

———. *The Mystery of the Coniunctio: Alchemical Image of Individuation: Lectures*. Studies in Jungian Psychology by Jungian Analysts. Toronto: Inner City Books, 1994.

———. The New God-Image: A Study of Jung's Key Letters Concerning the Evolution of the Western God-Image. Edited by Dianne D. Cordic and Charles Yates. Re-Release. Asheville, North Carolina: Chiron Publications, 2015.

Edinger, Edward F., and Deborah A. Wesley. *The Aion Lectures: Exploring the Self in C.G. Jung's Aion*. Studies in Jungian Psychology by Jungian Analysts. Willmet, IL: Inner City Books, 2013.

Emspak, Jesse. Contributions from Kimberly Hickok. "What Is Quantum Entanglement?" Space.com, March 16, 2022. https://www.space.com/31933-quantum-entanglement-action-at-a-distance.html.

Finch, Cora. "Stellar Fire: Carl Jung, a New England Family, and the Risk of Anecdote," n.d. http://web.archive.org/web/20080620085423/http://www.stellarfire.org/index.html#2.

Forsyth, Mark. *The Etymologicon: A Circular Stroll through the Hidden Connections of the English Language*. Berkley trade pbk. ed. New York: Berkley Books, 2012.

Galanter, Marc, William L. White, and Brooke D. Hunter. "Cross-Cultural Applicability of the 12-Step Model: A Comparison of Narcotics Anonymous in the USA and

Iran." *Journal of Addiction Medicine* 13, no. 6 (2019): 493–99.

Hamilton, Edith. *Mythology: Timeless Tales of Gods and Heroes.* 75th anniversary illustrated edition. New York: Black Dog & Leventhal Publishers, 2017.

Herrmann, Steven. *William James and C.G. Jung: Doorways to the Self.* Oberlin, OH: Analytical Psychology Press, 2021.

———. "Jaime de Angulo and C.G. Jung," 2014. Unpublished, shared with permission.

———. Donald Kalsched: The Inner World of Trauma, *The San Francisco Jung Institute Library Journal*, 19:2, 51-71, DOI: 10.1525/jung.1.2000.19.2.51.

Hollis, James. *Through the Dark Wood: Finding Meaning in the Second Half of Life.* Boulder, CO: Sounds True Publications, 2014.

James, William, and Bruce Kuklick. *Writings, 1902-1910.* The Library of America 38. New York: Literary Classics of the United States: Distributed to the trade in the U.S. and Canada by Viking, 1987.

Jung, C. G. *Alchemical Studies.* 1. Princeton, Bollingen paperback print. Paperback Editions of C. G. Jung's Writings / Transl. by R. F. C. Hull. Princeton, NJ: Princeton University Press, 1983.

———. *Collected Works of C.G. Jung, Volume 5: Symbols of Transformation.* Edited by R. F.C. Hull. Vol. 5. Princeton, NJ: Princeton University Press, 2014.

———. *Collected Works of C.G. Jung, Volume 9 (Part 1).* Edited by R. F.C. Hull. Vol. 9. Princeton, NJ: Princeton University Press, 2014.

―――. *Collected Works of C.G. Jung, Volume 9 (Part 2): Aion: Researches into the Phenomenology of the Self.* Edited by R. F.C. Hull. *Vol. 9ii.* Princeton, NJ: Princeton University Press, 2014.

―――. *Collected Works of C.G. Jung, Volume 10: Civilization in Transition.* Edited by R. F.C. Hull. Vol. 10. Princeton, NJ: Princeton University Press, 2014. https://doi.org/10.1515/9781400850976.

―――. *Collected Works of C.G. Jung, Volume 12: Psychology and Alchemy.* Edited by R. F.C. Hull. Vol. 12. Princeton, NJ: Princeton University Press, 2014. https://doi.org/10.1515/9781400850877.

―――. *Letters.* Bollingen Series, 95: 1-2. Princeton, N.J.: Princeton University Press, 1973.

―――. *Modern Man in Search of a Soul.* Translated by W. S. Dell and Cary F. Baynes. Eastford, CT: Martino Fine Books, 2021.

―――. *The Spirit in Man, Art, and Literature.* Bollingen Series 20. Princeton, NJ: Princeton University Press, 1995.

Jung, C. G. *C.G. Jung Speaking: Interviews and Encounters.* Princeton, NJ: Princeton University Press, 1977.

Jung, C. G., Gerhard Adler, and R. F. C. Hull. *Collected Works of C.G. Jung, Volume 6: Psychological Types.* Vol. 6. Collected Works of C.G. Jung. Princeton, NJ: Princeton University Press, 2014. https://www.jstor.org/stable/10.2307/j.ctt5hhqtj.

Jung, C. G., and Joseph Campbell. *The Portable Jung.* New York: Penguin Books, 1976.

Jung, C. G., and James L. Jarrett. *Jung's Seminar on Nietzsche's Zarathustra*. Abridged ed. Bollingen Series 99. Princeton, NJ Princeton University Press, 1998.

Jung, C. G., *Collected Works of C.G. Jung, Volume 4: Freud & Psychoanalysis*. Edited by R.F.C. Hull. Princeton, NJ: Princeton University Press, 2014.

———. *Collected Works of C.G. Jung, Volume 8: The Structure and Dynamics of the Psyche*. Edited by R.F.C. Hull. Vol. 8. Princeton, NJ: Princeton University Press, 2014.

———. *Collected Works of C.G. Jung, Volume 11: Psychology and Religion: West and East*. Edited by R.F.C. Hull. Vol. 11. Princeton, NJ: Princeton University Press, 2014.

———. *Collected Works of C.G. Jung, Volume 17: Development of the Personality*. Edited by R. F.C. Hull. Vol. 17. Princeton, NJ: Princeton University Press, 2024.

———. *Collected Works of C.G. Jung, Volume 18: The Symbolic Life*. Edited by R. F.C. Hull. Vol. 11. Princeton, NJ: Princeton University Press, 2024.

Jung, C. G., and Aniela Jaffé. *Memories, Dreams, Reflections*. Rev. ed. New York: Vintage Books, 1989.

Jung, Carl Gustav, and Richard Francis Carrington Hull. *Answer to Job*. Bollingen Series. Princeton, NJ: Princeton University Press, 2011.

Kalsched, Donald. *The Inner World of Trauma: Archetypal Defenses of the Personal Spirit*. Repr. London: Routledge, 1998.

Kurtz, Ernest, and Katherine Ketcham. *The Spirituality of Imperfection: Storytelling and the Journey to Wholeness*. New York: Bantam, 1994.

Koelsch, William A. "Incredible Day-Dream": Freud and Jung at Clark, 1909. Worcester, MA: The Friends of the Goddard Library, 1984.

Lattin, Don. *Distilled Spirits: Getting High, Then Sober, with a Famous Writer, a Forgotten Philosopher, and a Hopeless Drunk*. Berkeley, CA: University of California Press, 2012.

Lean, Garth. *Frank Buchman: A Life*. London: Constable, 1985.

Library of Congress: https://www.loc.gov/exhibits/freud/ex/131.html.

McCabe, Ian. *Carl Jung and Alcoholics Anonymous: The Twelve Steps as a Spiritual Journey of Individuation*. London: Karnac, 2015.

Melo, Walter and Costa de Resende, Pedro H. "The Impact of James' Varieties of Religious Experience on Jung's Work." *Journal of the American Psychological Association* 23, no. 1 (2020): 62–76.

Meister Eckhart and Houston Smith, *Meister Eckhart: The Essential Sermons, Commentaries, Treatises and Defense*, trans. Edmund Colledge and Bernard McGinn, New edition (New York: Paulist Press, 1981).

Neumann, Erich. *The Origins and History of Consciousness*. Bollingen Series 42. Princeton, NJ: Princeton University Press, 1970.

O., Mike. "The Roundtable of A.A. History," The Roundtable of A.A. History, January 10, 1998 (March 19, 2023). https://silkworth.net/alcoholics-anonymous/william-duncan-silkworth-md-1873-1951/.

Onions, Charles T., ed. *The Oxford Dictionary of English Etymology*. Repr. Oxford: Oxford University Press, 1996.

Otto, Rudolf. *The Idea of the Holy: An Inquiry into the Non-Rational Factor in the Idea of the Divine and Its Relation to the Rational*. A Galaxy Book GB14. New York: Oxford University Press, 1958.

"Physis Definition and Meaning | Collins English Dictionary," April 12, 2023. https://www.collinsdictionary.com/us/dictionary/english/physis.

Pollan, Michael. *How to Change Your Mind: What the New Science of Psychedelics Teaches Us about Consciousness, Dying, Addiction, Depression, and Transcendence*. New York: Penguin Press, 2018.

Praet, Danny. "'Explaining the Christianization of the Roman Empire. Older Theories and Recent Developments.'" *Sacris Erudiri. JA.A.rboek Voor Godsdienstgeschiedenis. A Journal on the Inheritance of Early and Medieval Christianity.*, no. 25 (1993 1992): 5–119.

Richardson, Robert Dale. *William James: In the Maelstrom of American Modernism a Biography*. Boston: Houghton Mifflin Co., 2006.

Schaberg, William H. *Writing "The Big Book": The Creation of A. A.* Las Vegas, NV: Central Recovery Press, 2019.

Schoen, David E. *The War of the Gods in Addiction: C.G. Jung, Alcoholics Anonymous, and Archetypal Evil*. Asheville, NC: Chiron Publications, 2020.

Schulte, Paul. *We Agnostics: How William James, Father of American Psychology, Advanced A Spiritual Solution to Addiction*. New York: Lantern Books, 2021.

Shamdasani, S. (1999). Memories, dreams, omissions. In P. Bishop (Ed.), *Jung in Contexts: A Reader* (pp. 33–50). Taylor & Frances/Routledge.

Siegel, Ethan. "The Three Meanings Of E=mc^2, Einstein's Most Famous Equation." Forbes. Accessed April 5, 2023. https://www.forbes.com/sites/startswithabang/2018/01/23/the-three-meanings-of-emc2-einsteins-most-famous-equation/.

Springer, John. "Bill W's 1934 Towns Hospital Belladonna Treatment." *Medium* (blog), April 15, 2020. https://medium.com/@johnspringer.architect/bill-ws-1934-towns-hospital-belladonna-treatment-5aafdc4252d.

Stein, Murray. *Transformation: Emergence of the Self*. Carolyn and Ernest Fay Series in Analytical Psychology, no 7. College Station, TX: Texas A&M university press, 1998.

Stein, Leslie and Lionel Corbett, Editors. *Psychedelics and Individuation: Essays by Jungian Analysts*. Ashville, N.C: Chiron Publications, 2023.

Twelve Steps and Twelve Traditions. New York: Alcoholics Anonymous World Services, 1981.

White, William L. *Slaying the Dragon: The History of Addiction Treatment and Recovery in America*. Second edition. Bloomington, IL: Chestnut Health Systems, 2014.

Williams, Michael A., Collett Cox, and Martin S. Jaffee, eds. *Innovation in Religious Traditions: Essays in the Interpretation of Religious Change*. Religion and Society 31. Berlin, New York: Mouton de Gruyter, 1992.

C

Index

based on the opposites 134
building blocks 138
cosmic meaning of 48
created objective existence 49
Eden myth of birth of 211
evolves alongside God-image
244
flower of a season 28
fundamental to material world
135
grows out of tension of opposites 216
interferes 115
is awareness of opposites 134
nervous system and 135
of compulsions greatest leap 225
the original sin 213
Cora Finch 56, 61, 62
counter-culture 29
craving 36, 150, 151
crisis 145, 153, 158, 249
Czar of Heaven 96, 104, 114, 124,
248
Czar of the Heavens. *See* Czar
of Heaven, metaphysical
approach

D

D.H. Lawrence 41
darkness
belly of the whale 176
individuals cut-off 246
integration, devil as spirit guide
182
loathsome human condition 165
not a barrier 5
of paradoxical God-image 246
only escape 6
suffered too long in 166
wisdom of darkness vanished
165

David E. Schoen 143
defects of character 69, 236, 238
delusion of control 158, 163, 216,
219, 222
depression 33, 207
Devil 169, 172, 176, 181, 193
misconstrued symbol 171
dilemma 6, 43, 57, 128, 139, 146,
150, 154, 165, 174, 191,
192, 209, 212, 213, 217,
218, 220, 233, 237, 250,
252
discipline 122, 172
doorway 251
shadow, subliminal 236
Doorways to the Self 16, 21, 23,
109, 186, 223, 244
driven 28, 38, 146, 158, 159, 248
drug-addict. *See* alcoholic

E

East
religion of introspective by
nature 118
Ebby 58, 61, 62, 89, 90, 91, 92,
128
Ebby Thacher
goes to New Mexico with
Rowland 61
helps Bill sober up 62
inspired response to Wilson 90
Eden 141, 179, 211, 217, 220, 222
Edward Edinger
Jungian author and analyst 79
ego
becoming conscious of itself in
Garden 213
birth of, symbolized by Fall 211
brings unconscious to light 243
complex relationship with the
Self 209

psychological construct 91
relative nature of 112
relieved of metaphysical
    restraints 131
separation from 96
shadowy half of 246
shape retreats 126
Wilson splits in his story 254
Wilson's consciousness regarding
    251
Wilson's never made the final
    leap 251
Wilson's reconciliation of 91
gods as a psychic factor 110, 116,
going native 30
good and evil
    an insoluble dilemma 173
Grand Canyon 45
Great Reality 95, 104, 112, 136,
    160, 256. *See* objective
    psyche
greeters 179

H

healing 5, 24, 32, 164, 166
    magic art of Shaman 164
Henry James Sr
    William James' father 16
hero's journey 123, 153
Herrmann. *See* Steven Herrmann
higher types. *See* neurosis
highest and lowest 254
holy of holies 180

I

impoverishment of symbolism 79,
    107
inadequate conception 114
Indians of the Great Plains 155

individuation
    as a new myth 79
    based on problem of opposites
        131
    basic points, Edinger 80
    goal of analytical method 27
    reqires discrimination of
        shadow 236
Individuation
    heroic task, Atonement 221
inflated ego 200, 201, 204
inner resource
    Wilson's conception of the
        transcendent function.
        See transcendent function,
        relativity of God-image
insoluble conflict 153, 212
insoluble conflicts 250
instinct 159, 167, 181, 234, 251
intangible thirst 150, 151, 208
intoxication
    a spiritual experience 36
intuition 9, 64, 124, 154
inventory 38, 69, 104, 237, 238
ism 175, 181

J

Jaime de Angulo
    adopts Achumawi myth 32
    Bay Area anthropologist and
        author. *See* Achumawi,
        Tony Lujan, Mountain Lake
    buys land east of Mt. Shasta 30
    goes to Bollingen 40
    he died so that we could live 52
    inflated ego due to drug-use 38
    lives and dies like a typical
        alcoholic 51
    model for Jung's understanding
        of addiction 36
    religious outlook upon life 30

272

prototype 145
psyche
  accords to structure of universe
    135
  and enantiodromia 192
  and transcendent function 182
  change in first 85
  diabolical elements of 226
  dynamic within 37
  dynamism of cosmos within 135
  inner world, opposed to physis
    84
  neurosis and a split within 173
  polaristic structure of 163
  problem of opposites in 132
  same as soul 83
  timeless 28
psychedelic mushroom 31
psychic change. *See* entire psychic
  change
psychic factors 108
psychoanalysis. *See* Sigmund
  Freud
psychological approach 10, 27,
  105, 109, 110, 114, 154,
  172
psychological functions
  God and the Devil as 181
  psychological law 188–190
psychological perspective
  way to adopt the primitive mindset 37
Psychological Types 36, 68, 109,
  111, 121, 125, 131, 132,
  170, 173, 245
  chapter on William James 24

Q

quantum entanglement 190

R

radical empiricism 19
  injecting experience with personal
  meaning 19
Ralph Waldo Emerson
  William James' godfather 16
Ramayana 132
recovery 6, 8, 9, 53, 69, 83, 85, 92,
  122, 132, 145, 152, 175, 192
  living myth without knowing it
  77
regressive analysis 37, 39, 52
relative 93, 114, 126, 170
relativity of the God-image 111,
  112, 113, 115, 116, 127
religion
  Freudian view, unresolved trauma
  24
religious attitude
  shared among mystics and Eastern
  gurus 110
religious conversion 16, 81
religious function 78, 111
religious images
  treat neuroses 19
religious statement 83
resentment. See inventory, Step
  Four
restored to sanity. *See* Step Two
rhizome 28, 29, 32, 35, 80, 129
Rowland Hazard
  Africa and New Mexico 59
  Jung's patient in 1926, right after
  Africa 56
  never joins A.A. 64
  Oxford Group curcuit speaker 60

S

Schaberg
  William Schaberg 11, 65, 66, 67,
  265